PENGUIN BUSINESS
ACHIEVING MEANINGFUL SUCCESS

Dr Vivek Mansingh is a global leader, entrepreneur, author, technology visionary, innovator and widely followed international speaker. He is a mentor par excellence and is in pursuit of 'Mentoring a Million'. He holds six US patents and has made vital contributions to two books on technology. He has had the privilege of working with Bill Hewlett, David Packard, Steve Jobs, Michael Dell and John Chambers.

Currently a general partner at YourNest VC Fund, he has incubated many start-ups and sits on the board of several for-profit and non-profit global organizations. Previously, he held management positions at HP and Fujitsu in Silicon Valley, and founded ATTI (Aavid) in the US, which went in for an IPO. He returned to India, and served as president at Cisco, Dell R&D, Ishoni Networks and Portal Software.

Dr Mansingh is a gold medallist from NIT Allahabad, obtained his PhD from Queen's University, Canada, and did his executive management at Stanford University. He was listed in the National Who's Who for the US in the year 2000. He also received the Chanakya Leadership Award in 2012 and was named IT Man of the Year, India, 2016, by Enterprise Connect, US.

His philanthropy programmes include emergency and eye-care hospitals for the poor.

Rachna Thakurdas has published several books. Her debut novel, *Dating, Diapers and Denial*, remained a bestseller for over a year. Her novel *Band, Baaja, Boys* has been adapted into a web series called *Mannphodgunj Ki Binny*. She has also published her diaries, written during her battle with breast cancer, in a book called *Mum's Gotta Live*.

She holds a master's degree in psychology and has worked in L&D with Tata Motors, Infosys and Dell. The *New Indian Express* hailed her as 'part of the new wave of genuinely funny, smart and self-aware women writers in the country'.

ADVANCE PRAISE FOR THE BOOK

'Every reader, irrespective of profession or age, will be able to pick up some golden nuggets from the book to improve his or her life'—N.R. Narayana Murthy, founder, Infosys

'A superbly interesting, inspiring and practical book for everyone; each page of this book has at least one idea that one can apply immediately. You can never be too young or too old to realize your potential'—Rajan Anandan, former head, Google, Microsoft and Dell

'We all need mentors. Instead of making your own mistakes, learn from mentors; that's less painful! Vivek's invaluable book can be your lifetime mentor'—John Chambers, ex-chairman, Cisco

'Immediately after Tenzing Norgay and Edmund Hillary scaled Mount Everest, there was a flood of people replicating their feat. That's the power of role models that Dr Mansingh's book highlights. His book will be an amazing mentor for any reader'—Dr Devi Shetty, founder, Narayana Health

'You need a guru or mentor to succeed and realize your potential. This extremely beautiful book can be your mentor'—Mohandas Pai, chairman, Manipal Education, and Aarin Capital

'I have read numerous books by Robin Sharma, Anthony Robbins and Stephen Covey, to name a few. However, this book is different and is like having a personal mentor. I am sure millions will get real-life mentoring from this book!'—Manoj Jhanji, co-founder, Kolektive Ventures

'Whether it is listening to his speech or having a conversation with him or reading this book, you won't be left disappointed . . . I can vouch for it; you get a 1000 per cent return on the Rs 300 you invest in this book. Get ready to be infected!'—Pradeep B., ex-CEO and managing editor, *siliconindia*

'This book takes on the role of a mentor in inspiring us and influencing our personal development by transforming us into leaders'—Vani Kola, founder and MD, Kalaari Capital

'Vivek's book is a powerful mentor in the form of a book. It illustrates the significance of holistic success and the power of big goals, and shows a path to become the best version of yourself to achieve your goals. The book will help people of all ages'—Manoj Kohli, MD, Softbank India

'Vivek's book is a contemporary rendition of India's ancient heritage: how to be a fully engaged, well-rounded karma-yogi in today's chaotic world. His message resonates because it is authentic; Vivek practises what he preaches'—Swati and Ramesh Ramanathan, founders, Jana Group

'This book coalesces illustrations and experiences into pragmatic and insightful concepts and practices to help one become the best possible version of oneself . . . and is therefore relevant to everyone'—Vinita Bali, former MD, Britannia

'I love the wheel of goals and being a better version of yourself. A beautifully structured, extremely important book for everyone'—T.N. Hari, founder, Artha School of Entrepreneurship, author and angel investor

'Dr Mansingh has a way of making the book feel like a conversation you're having with a mentor, further motivating you to go after those dreams! Definitely recommend this one!'—Shefali Prakash, assistant director, Deloitte, UK

'Delightful reading, it is a page-turner. You learn something new in each chapter. Vivek Mansingh is already a successful mentor and now is a brilliant writer too'—Shubhra Sinha, member, board of advisers, Dataworkz, USA

'*Achieving Meaningful Success* is one of the best books I have read in recent times. It will impact in a good way anyone who reads it. Be it entrepreneurs, professionals, students or anyone'—Gokul Muralidharan, founder, Argoid, USA

'I always thought that our experience is our best teacher. However, with this book, my view stands changed. I will keep this book on my desk as my companion till I achieve my own version of meaningful success'—Sujay Dutta, analytics leader, Canada

'Amazingly well-written, as if you are listening to the author. The book provides lifelong learnings'—Mudit Dandwate, founder, Dozee

'The book is addictive. You read one chapter and another and another and so on . . . Dr Mansingh's experience and guidance are laid out in a very simple and easily understandable process'—Ashok Karani, senior director, global software, GE Healthcare

'Just like a conversation with a mentor would motivate and guide you, reading the book makes you feel a sense of optimism and confidence at every step of your personal and professional life'—Swati Sharma, co-founder and chief strategy officer, Thriwe

'Dr Mansingh has hit it out of the park, as he has always does. Once you start reading this book, you cannot put it down. It is an amazingly well-written book, which provides the blueprint of achieving meaningful, all-round success'—Sunil Menon, Telstra

'The most relevant 300 pages that you need to read NOW! Dr Mansingh has artistically woven an immensely valuable knowledge artifact that is timeless. In my belief, this book will add value to a person at any age'—Siddhartha Chandra, data scientist, Collective[i], USA

'A fail-safe recipe for success. Most of the self-development books turn out to be unconnected, unsolicited advice and hence remain unread midway through. But *Achieving Meaningful Success* is a welcome change. It is inspirational and highly motivating'—Asokan Sattanathan, founder, Aahaa Technologies

'Everyone needs and deserves mentorship irrespective of age or profession, but not everyone has access to it. This book helps you bridge that gap. I found great mentorship in this book'—Shreya Punj, Read Better

ACHIEVING MEANINGFUL SUCCESS

Unleash the Power of ME!

DR VIVEK MANSINGH

with RACHNA THAKURDAS

PENGUIN
BUSINESS

An imprint of Penguin Random House

PENGUIN BUSINESS

USA | Canada | UK | Ireland | Australia
New Zealand | India | South Africa | China | Singapore

Penguin Business is part of the Penguin Random House group of companies
whose addresses can be found at global.penguinrandomhouse.com

Published by Penguin Random House India Pvt. Ltd
4th Floor, Capital Tower 1, MG Road,
Gurugram 122 002, Haryana, India

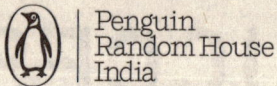

First published in Penguin Business by Penguin Random House India 2022

ISBN 9780143456469

Sketches by Suresh Huidrom

Typeset in Adobe Caslon Pro by Manipal Technologies Limited, Manipal
Printed at Thomson Press India Ltd, New Delhi

www.penguin.co.in

I am a product of my mother's inspiration and prayers,
my father's belief and value system,
my teachers' and mentors' guidance,
and
my passion for achieving meaningful success!

This book is dedicated to my wife, Preeti,
for her unconditional love and support.
To my children, Anant, Anoosha and Ayush,
for their constant encouragement, and
to my granddaughter, Iraa.

All earnings from this book will be donated to
Sadguru Netra Chikitsalaya, Chitrakoot,
towards eye care for the poor.

Contents

Author's Note

They say life doesn't come with an instruction manual. But *this book is an amazing instruction manual for life*! And if you read it with the instructions given here, it will be an excellent lifetime mentor through all phases of your life.

I have an extremely strong conviction in the value of mentorship and the methods to achieving meaningful success that I have followed. When I address audiences across the world, I am asked how I have applied these methods to achieve meaningful success and if I could recommend only one book on self-improvement, which would that be? This book is an answer to these questions. In fact, not just me, thousands of people whom I have mentored over the years have benefited from the methods of achieving success that this book covers. *I believe everyone needs and deserves a mentor*. This book can be your lifelong mentor and help you succeed in your career and life. *My dream is to 'Mentor A Million' people through this book.*

Why this book?

It's similar to an adept lifetime mentor faithfully by your side to guide you through various stages of life. The ideas shared are relevant to people of ages fifteen years onwards, from high school students to senior professionals to CEOs.

It guides you in achieving meaningful success and *leading a purposeful life through multidimensional and balanced life goals*, which are the key to happiness, fulfilment and a regret-free life.

The first part of the book focuses on defining the person you aspire to be. It shows you a step-by-step process to define the aspirational life goals that will help you achieve meaningful success, including amazing professional success. *The second part is about becoming the best version of yourself and worthy enough to realize your aspirations.*

It gives you processes to structure your plans and roadmaps to guide critical skill development for succeeding in your professional and personal life. It's more like a carpenter's toolkit than a book.

It is in the realm of 'achievable'. It's not about leaps of success made by those who are one in a million or inconceivable accounts of rare success stories. The sheer attainability of the lessons is its unique point.

Many books in this genre are authored by academicians, trainers and consultants who may not have real-life experience and may not have 'been there, done that'. The ideas shared in this book come from the real-life experiences of the author.

It is packed with anecdotes, insights and tips from several hugely successful, world-class individuals whom I admire. *These are exclusive interviews done for this book.* These people have won tremendous acclaim and achieved meaningful success by upholding beliefs similar to those discussed in the book.

Several people, who have benefited from my mentoring with the process and techniques described in this book, have shared their experiences and how these have helped them. I am sure you will relate to some very well.

How to benefit from this book

The methods to success given in the book are trusted and tested. *But implementation is key.* You have to start doing what it suggests with all the discipline that you can muster.

First, read the book. It flows very simply with stories and makes for an engaging read. You may find some incidents from my life repeated in different chapters. It is done in order to make each chapter complete and independent, and reinforce the ideas with examples from my life.

Then, read each chapter again by placing yourself at the centre, and ponder on how it applies to you.

Then reread the chapter on defining your wheel of goals. Take a notepad and draw your own wheel of goals.

Write down your long-term and short-term goals, and specific actions to be taken.

Remember, you have to first define the person you aspire to be.

Once you have defined clear goals, let the magic of passion kick in. Become obsessed with your goals.

The content in the rest of the chapters will help you become the best version of yourself and achieve success beyond your dreams.

Continue to review your progress, preferably monthly, and tweak actions if you wish to get closer to your desired results.

Once a year, thoroughly review your progress, **read the book again and create new goals as needed**. As you read the book again and again, you will derive *new wisdom each time*.

As life changes, shape and reshape your goals to match the changing contexts.

Then act and give it the best you have. *You will be amazed to see how much potential you have and how far you can go.*

Have questions after reading the book?

This book is designed to be your life mentor and will guide you through various stages of life. If you have questions after reading the book, please submit them at the website **www.vivekmansingh.com** or social media sites mentioned at the end of the book, to receive ongoing mentoring, free of cost and any obligations. You will also find a lot of supporting information, talks and interviews on my website that will motivate you through your journey.

The ball is in your court; make it happen!

Prologue

It was November 1962. A steam engine, puffing huge clouds of black smoke, hauled in ten or so obedient coaches at the Fatehpur railway station. The train's halt was going to be only for a few minutes.

The platform was teeming with people as usual, but today, quite peculiarly, there were mostly ladies. They were clutching the pleats of their sarees while almost sprinting, their slippers slapping against their heels. No, not to board the train. A small boy half-walked, half-ran to keep pace with his mother's long strides.

The train windows were open, and through them, one could spot bare, wooden-planked berths. Seated on them were soldiers. Dressed in army fatigues, their belongings packed in olive-green holdalls and trunks, they were on their way to an important and urgent assignment: war.

There had been a series of violent border skirmishes after the 1959 Tibetan uprising, when India had granted asylum to the Dalai Lama. The government had put in place a defensive forward policy from 1960 to hinder Chinese military patrols and logistics. As per the policy, the government placed outposts along the disputed McMahon Line at the India–China border. A war between China and India had broken out at these points.

The woman and her son stopped near one of the train's coach windows. She thrust a packet into the hands of a soldier. It was a cardigan she had knitted—a beautiful maroon one with a fascinating crossed cable-knit pattern—perfection that she always aimed for. Since much of the fighting was taking place in harsh mountain conditions, entailing large-scale combat at altitudes of over 4000 metres, all these ladies, led by my mother, had knitted cardigans for the soldiers. They had also packed sweet and savoury snacks in boxes.

The train windows were lined with ladies handing over the packages to the brave sons of the motherland.

In a few moments, the engine sounded its horn, and the coaches jiggled in preparation to leave. The small six-year-old boy stood there, transfixed. *That incident and his mother, a woman of strong character, would leave a deep mark on his life*.

CAPTURE YOUR ASPIRATIONS

MY JOURNEY

ONE

My Journey to Meaningful Success: Lessons Learnt

'Our life is not just for staying alive, but in finding something purposeful to live for.'
—Dr Vivek Mansingh

I am a believer. I believe that anyone, however humble their beginnings and whatever obstacles life throws at them, can achieve meaningful success and lead a purpose-filled life. I believe that if a boy from a small, largely agrarian town can go on to work with David Packard and Bill Hewlett (Hewlett-Packard), Steve Jobs (Apple), Michael Dell (Dell) and John Chambers (Cisco)—probably the only person in the world to work with each of these distinguished personalities—anyone can!

I want to make it clear, though, that I am no Narayana Murthy or Rahul Dravid. I am a simple person like you, who has realized his potential and achieved meaningful success. ***Meaningful success is when a person sets his/her***

multidimensional balanced aspirational life goals and achieves them. Time and again, it has been seen that achieving meaningful success gives lasting fulfilment and happiness, and helps one avoid regrets in life.

But before I share lessons from my life, I would like to narrate my story. I strongly believe that stories are the most powerful form of human communication and telling my story is the best way to illustrate the concept of meaningful success.

On a curiously interesting date, 3-4-'56, I was born to Udai and Rekha Mansingh. It was a home birth at Fatehpur, a small town in Uttar Pradesh. I grew up in a sort of joint family. While everyone lived in their own houses next to each other, we were connected not only by physical proximity but also by love. The group of cousins who were playmates, friends and confidants felt free to eat in any house and sleep anywhere!

I studied at the Government Intermediate College, Fatehpur, a modest Hindi-medium school with bare-bones facilities. My cousins in Allahabad, Lucknow and Kanpur, all bigger cities, unlike me, had access not only to ice cream but also to an English-medium school and much better education. It never bothered me, though. My eyes were set on being the best and, in defining what was 'best', the idea of role models was instilled early in my life by my mother. She nudged me to look up to my uncles and cousins who were notching academic and professional wins.

I completed my undergraduate studies in Mechanical Engineering from Motilal Nehru National Institute of Technology (MNNIT) Allahabad and, despite being a largely truant student on account of my chock-a-block extracurricular calendar, I won the academic gold medal for graduating at the top of the class. I played badminton for my engineering college as well as Allahabad University and was a keen singer, with a penchant for old Hindi movie songs. My singing was inspired by my younger sister, Surabhi, who is a wonderful and decorated singer. I also played at tournaments for tennis, cricket and bridge. I really can't remember when I would sleep! Through this experience, I learnt that a well-rounded day's schedule is to the mind what a healthy diet is to the body.

My first job was at JK Synthetics in Kota, Rajasthan. I continued to work hard and play hard too. It helped that the company's club was right opposite the bachelors' hostel! I would play billiards, cricket and badminton there. I sang at events. Egged on by friends, I contested the elections for the post of the president of the club. Surprisingly, and despite being a newbie, I won! I was becoming aware of my innate leadership skills and relishing using them.

From there, I went to Queen's University, Canada, to do my MS in Mechanical Engineering on a McLaughlin Fellowship that covered 100 per cent of the cost of my education. It was quite the transition! Here I was in a shiny new campus, a sort of bumpkin who'd never seen a computer in his life. But I had a huge fire in my belly. I craved and greedily claimed every piece of learning on offer. It typically takes people about two years to do their Masters but I finished mine in fourteen months.

I rewarded myself by travelling through Europe. I must have visited around ten countries; life's learning from each was sparkling and incredible. After that, I embarked on my PhD at Queen's University, Canada, and completed it in 1986. During the time of writing my PhD thesis, I also worked as an adjunct professor at Lehigh University, Pennsylvania, USA.

Around that time, I met my soulmate, Preeti, at my cousin's wedding in India. We got married and started life together in Bethlehem, Pennsylvania. We welcomed our first son, Anant, and life was rosy and comfortable. We loved to toss our stuff in our car and explore nearby cities and tourist attractions. The baby didn't fuss at all; I guess he, too, enjoyed those impromptu vacations!

My career, I would say, started in 1987, with Hewlett-Packard in Cupertino, California. I did some leading-edge technology design work for HP Computers, published several technical papers, and started my innovation and patent journey by filing my first patent for HP. In addition, I got a chance to interact with the legendary founders. Once, on a trip from San Jose to Colorado Springs on HP's private jet, as I was waiting at the HP terminal at San Jose airport, I spotted David Packard and Bill Hewlett walking in. I was floored when David Packard told me that he was going to make coffee at the coffee machine and asked me if I wanted one. During the flight, he asked me to sit between him and Bill. I was ecstatic! Then they asked me what my two biggest achievements at HP were so far. I described my invention (patent) and a paper I wrote in the HP journal about the airflow and thermal computer simulation (the largest in the world at that time) that I had carried out using the supercomputer Cray. They listened intently and asked me a lot of questions. As the flight landed, I asked them what was the one skill I should develop to enrich my career. Their response, which I will always treasure, was: *continuous learning and becoming the best version of myself.* What wonderful leaders, such down-to-earth icons who established HP as one of the top corporations in the world, kind souls who gave away most of their wealth to Stanford University!

Having been conditioned to goal-setting from my student days, I was thinking about my next set of goals. You see, while one is studying, goals are simple: *do your best, get good grades and get a good job.* It's clear and unambiguous. But when one exits college and begins a career, goals dissipate. In their place, one becomes *opportunity-driven*, without even realizing it! At this point, it is important to be acutely aware that a fresh round of goal-setting is needed.

'The world steps aside for a person who knows where he's headed.'

—Mahatma Gandhi

I, too, believe in the leviathan power of goals.

At that time, my trajectory was probably the same as thousands of others with the same background as mine. Except that I had set one singularly different goal. My goal was to become financially independent by the time I turned forty. This was the goal of a thirty-year-old who didn't have a green card, nor any family-inherited wealth, and the responsibility of a newborn son and a wife. I wrote down the goal in clear, measurable terms: *What is my definition of financial independence at the age of forty?*

The power of having a goal and writing it down is that it tells us, in no uncertain terms, what is to be achieved. There is no aimless meandering when your goal is firmly committed to paper. Half the job was done. I had a goal. *But how the hell was I going to achieve it?* I racked my brain for days. Finally, I made a decision—I'd innovate and come up with a product that I could license to a company. The idea consumed me. I would think about it all the time after my day job at HP. I would flirt with hundreds of ideas. Some of them popped into my head during the night. I wouldn't dare to sleep lest I forgot them. *It was such an all-consuming passion!* Preeti suggested that I keep a notepad and pen by my bedside and jot down whatever idea came to me so that my mind could calm down and I could go back to sleep. My weekends and evenings were spent in my garage tinkering with these ideas. Within a year, I had invented an instrument (not related to my work at HP), patented it and licensed it to Cambridge Accusense, a Boston-based company. I started earning royalties on it, which would go on for seventeen years. By *thinking outside the box* and *innovating*, I was well on my way to achieving my goal of financial independence.

From HP, I moved to Fujitsu in 1991 with the clear objective of garnering sales and marketing experience. Mind you, it meant taking a position lower than my current one! But I didn't flinch. I was clear that I needed to round out my professional profile. Hence, sales experience was needed. I led a team of R&D engineers, marketing managers and sales managers in the US and Japan, to establish Fujitsu's multimillion-dollar microelectronics business. Our second son, Ayush, was born during this period. My eagerness to learn more wasn't subsiding, only growing. So, I enrolled in and completed an executive management programme from Stanford University.

The next goal was to become *number one in my field in the US and to start my own company*. I set up ATTI, an engineering services company, from scratch, in 1997. This was in Santa Clara, California. Soon, it blazed a trail, leading the pack with clients such as Apple,

Cisco, HP and Juniper Networks. During this time, *I got the chance to work with Steve Jobs* on the iMac, the first product from Apple after Steve became Apple's CEO for the second time. Being passionate about design, Steve challenged us to design the iMac with very demanding design specifications and without any fan. After a lot of analysis and creative thinking, we came up with an innovative solution, which was appreciated and highlighted by Steve himself when he launched the product with a lot of fanfare. An immensely proud moment for us was when we received a personalized note on a big poster of the iMac saying, '*To Vivek and team, thank you so much for your help, we couldn't have done it without you.*' Innovation and excellence at work!

I had reached the number one spot in my field in the US, had six US patents in my name and was a star speaker at technical conferences. I must have addressed technical seminars at more than 100 top universities and technology companies around the world—Intel, HP, General Motors, Sun, Silicon Graphics, Mercedes, to name a few. Educational publisher McGraw Hill approached me to write a book. I started it, but developed carpal tunnel syndrome (a medical condition that causes weakness and pain in the hand due to repeated pressure on a nerve in the wrist), which made it extremely painful to type, so it was converted into a chapter in a McGraw Hill handbook for electronic systems design.

ATTI was fully merged into Aavid and became its R&D and services arm. Aavid became an engineering design software and thermal products company with revenues of over $350 million a year. It was listed as one of *Fortune* magazine's 100 fastest-growing companies in the US in 1999. Apart from my other roles, I particularly enjoyed my role as the spokesman for Aavid on Wall Street. *I was pursuing excellence with passion and loving the fruits of it.*

Then, life threw me a curveball: my mother, who had been my beacon and stronghold, was diagnosed with end-stage renal failure. My brother and I rushed her to Stanford Hospital but sadly, after all the tests, we were told that she had just six months to live. We were devastated. *Without batting an eyelid, I decided to return to India with my family.* This was one of the biggest and most difficult decisions of my life, and was possible only because Preeti agreed to the move without a moment of hesitation. So did Anant and Ayush, even though they were leaving behind friends, school and the only life they knew. Looking back, I am so happy I—rather, we—could do it.

It was extremely gratifying to be in India with my mother; to watch her play with her grandchildren and share special moments with the rest of us. This leaf from my life's book teaches us that **different goals take precedence in different phases of life**. For me, taking care of my parents had always been right at the top on the list of my life goals.

You know, I find lists like 'The Top Fifty Richest People in the World' inappropriate and misleading. They wrongly equate success with money. Why can't we share stories of people who have achieved meaningful success, especially with the younger generation, to inspire them to seek meaningful success? Life cannot be about chasing money only; in fact, 'profits' at both an individual and an organizational level should be only *one* of the objectives in a cluster of objectives.

On the work front, India was a mixed bag. My first job was with Jasmine Networks, an optical networking company from Silicon Valley. However, in 2001, with the big Wall Street collapse, its funding dried up. I had to close operations and was left in a precarious position! Looking back, I am grateful for this failure of sorts. It filled me with more purpose and determination.

Then, I joined Ishoni Networks India as managing director. I led the development of a platform of embedded software for Ishoni's broadband and VoIP system on a chip. Ishoni also faced the brunt of a financial meltdown and was acquired by Philips in 2003. Then, I moved on to my next professional challenge, Portal Software, as an MD.

On the family front, the sad but inevitable happened: my mother passed away in May 2003. Her demise was peaceful with her husband, three children and their spouses by her side. She lived for more than two years— much longer than the six months that the Stanford doctors had estimated and we thoroughly cherished those years with her. One of her parting messages to me was that she felt that she'd lived for ten years instead of two. My siblings and I were united in our goal to make her last days as comfortable and emotionally rich as we possibly could.

My father, though never one to admit it, seemed to have lost his purpose in life. His anchor and his mainstay, my mother, had gone. We had to do something. My younger brother, Saket, had a brainwave—to start social-welfare projects in Fatehpur and involve him in them. One project's goal was to get corrective surgery done for handicapped children. It infused a spark in my father and gave him a new joy in life. I joined wholeheartedly and supported the project. My happiness grew on seeing him thrive with his newfound zeal. *Over three hundred children were helped through this initiative; most walked for the first time in their lives after surgery.*

At Portal Software, I led the development of Portal's revenue management software products. Portal was acquired by Oracle in 2005. By this point, I had joined the ranks of senior leadership. I learnt that as a leader, I needed to win trust and touch the hearts of my team members before asking for their hands. I strove to genuinely know and connect with people. I am proud that there was almost no attrition in my direct reports during my entire career; this meant more than the product or revenue wins, I must say. Leadership skills at work. What 'meaningful success' stands for never left my consciousness. I was still the eager learner that I was two decades ago. I was also passionate about doing my best in my career and giving back to society.

I joined Dell India's R&D Centre in 2005 as the country head and was one of the four members of the Dell India leadership team, managing 25,000+ Dell employees and over $1 billion in sales. I led the development of Dell's server hardware and systems management software products for global markets. As I reflect on this phase of my career, *I cherish my rewarding interactions with Michael Dell.* Every conversation with him was packed with learning! He respected me most, among other things, for making Dell India the most innovative R&D site, with the highest number of innovations (patentable ideas), among Dell China, Taiwan and Singapore. I promised him that I would develop an engineer at Dell India who would go on to win the Michael Dell Award for Innovation in fewer than five years. *He was thrilled and congratulated me when I achieved this goal in three years.* During one of Michael Dell's Bangalore visits, we were invited for dinner by Azim Premji (Wipro chairman and philanthropist) at his house. It was an astonishing lesson in humility to see Mrs Premji herself serving food to all of us.

Then, I joined Cisco India as president of the Collaboration & Communications Technology Group in 2010. I led global teams for developing innovative global collaboration and cloud-based products. Cisco's collaboration product portfolio had $4.5 billion revenue per year then. During this time, *my learnings from John Chambers, chairman and CEO, were phenomenal.* My last meeting with John was at his lavish home in Palo Alto, California. He gave me a copy of his book *Connecting the Dots* with a remarkable note saying, 'Vivek, congratulations for many successes . . . hope we find several companies to work in together.' After the meeting, he walked me to my car. The car wasn't parked in his porch; it was a good 400 metres down his tree-lined driveway! When I told him that I would walk myself out, he shared that he was with French President Emmanuel Macron the previous week and after the meeting, Macron walked him to his car. He said he had learnt a lesson in humility and wanted to follow it himself. This and many other amazing interactions with John have taught me *leadership skills, the power of mentoring, the importance of forging genuine relationships for success and humility.*

When I retired from Cisco India, I was offered a position with Cisco in the US as there is no retirement age there. However, my father was over eighty years old at that time; hence, I decided to stay in India and spend some quality time with him. *I am proud that once again I gave higher priority to relationships and taking care of a parent than to career and money.*

It was time to go back to my wheel of goals, evaluate my life situation and create a ten-year plan for this new phase of life. This exercise guided me to arrive at the goals of helping create successful global product start-ups from India, mentoring millions of young people in our country, and giving back to the less fortunate. *The goal of mentoring millions encouraged me to conceive the 'Mentor A Million' initiative and write this book*.

Reinventing myself and tweaking my career path several times, from global expert in electronics cooling to country head and software leader to mentor and leader in the start-up and venture capital world, I can look back with satisfaction at where my career goals have led me. Clear career goals have not only helped me notch up fascinating milestones but also tide over several bumps.

Throughout my career, I have happily shared my life's experiences on many platforms and with audiences of diverse backgrounds. I have addressed people around the world on topics such as Electronics Cooling, Cloud Computing, the Internet of Things, Leadership, Excellence, Innovation and Achieving Meaningful Success. The audiences have hailed not only from the world of professionals but also from other walks of life, and include students and members of Rotary Clubs across India. I am also proud of having shared my experiences and learnings with Indian army officers at several border outposts, including those in Ladakh, Sikkim, Arunachal Pradesh and Rajasthan.

In my individual capacity and as a board member of several for-profit and non-profit organizations, I am striving to give back to society. My goal is to give back not a small fraction of my time and resources but something significant. I am actively driving several programmes for the underprivileged in Fatehpur with the goal of helping and empowering over 1 lakh (1,00,000) people in the next five years.

Coming back to family, in 2016, my elder son Anant gave us a beautiful gift. He found his soulmate Anoosha and they had a wonderful wedding. Preeti and I were delighted to welcome Anoosha as our first daughter. It was very special that my father was able to attend the wedding and bless the new couple, even though he had started developing some health issues.

Life changes colours, as we know. On a sad note, my father and inspirer passed away peacefully in 2018 surrounded by his children, their spouses and his grandchildren. We thoroughly enjoyed his company, his poetry and visiting various places with him in his last few years. He worked hard to help the less fortunate until his last day. *He taught us that the way to earn the respect of one's own children is by loving unconditionally and serving others*.

I am enjoying my new role as a general partner at YourNest VC Fund and board member at several Indian and international companies. It allows me to mentor and advise many founders and start-ups. My goal is to help create at least three unicorns, more-than-one-billion-dollar market capitalization companies, that will help

India's economic development and create at least 50,000 jobs over the years.

My home office is my sanctuary. The plaques and mementoes that Preeti and I have placed there remind us of the journey we have covered. I feel chuffed looking at all of them. Winning Information Technology Man of the Year, India (2016) was particularly special. My six US patents in the field of hardware technology are a source of pride. So are my contributions to two books and more than a hundred technical papers. My award for National Who's Who for the United States (2000) and Chanakya Leadership Award of India for National Achievers (2012) beam down on me, encouraging me to be an even better version of myself.

God has been kind and has blessed me with *meaningful and fulfilling success*. I have largely remained joyful through the ups and downs of my life. Although I have never chased money, I have done well in my profession, received a few prestigious awards, achieved my financial goals, live in one of the most exclusive communities of Bangalore and drive a Mercedes. I have joyfully done my duty to my parents and cherish their blessings. My sons have gone to the best colleges in the United States, are doing the jobs they love in some of the best companies in the world and are on their own path to meaningful success. I have travelled to many countries, lead a healthy lifestyle, treasure my relationships, have mentored thousands of people and many start-ups, and given back to the community in a significant way, making a difference to thousands of less fortunate people. But as it is said:

> '*Life is a journey, not a destination.*'
> —Ralph Waldo Emerson

By the grace of god, I have enjoyed the journey of my life so far as much as the destination. The lessons I share in my talks have benefited thousands of people and have been appreciated by thousands of my mentees. I am attempting to put those lessons in this book in the hope that they inspire the reader to identify and pursue meaningful success in life. I have reaped the fruits of a life built around balanced goals pursued with the process, techniques and skill development shared in this book. You see, *there is no Rewind button in life*. There is no Undo feature! Hence, it is critical to plan now so that there are no regrets later.

In this overcomplicated world, the simple lessons in this book offer a blueprint for achieving meaningful success in life. They will guide you steadfastly; not just towards occasional success but to multiplied successes. **This book is designed to be your life mentor**, showing you the path to *achieving meaningful success through all the stages of your life.*

Achieving Meaningful Success is a box of seeds I wish to sprinkle on fertile minds. Who knows, a leaf from my story can be the seed for yours!

Key Learnings

1. I am a simple man, my name does not appear in the list of richest people or most successful CEOs but, in all humility, I believe I have achieved meaningful success by leading a multidimensional and balanced life. I am not sure how many CEOs would have the courage to leave their well-paying jobs and the lifestyle that came with those jobs, to move from the US to India at the drop of a hat, to take care of their parents. That too, with two young US-born children and without any job in hand, which meant building life from square one! ***Meaningful success is about achieving what is meaningful to you***.

2. I have shared my life story as a case study. The strategies I have used in my life are right here in these pages to help you achieve meaningful success. By following them, I am sure you will succeed beyond your dreams, be proud of your life and enjoy the destination as well as the journey of life.

DEFINE YOUR GOALS

TWO

Define Your Wheel of Goals: Capture Your Aspirations!

'Define who you aspire to be, then become that person!'
—Dr Vivek Mansingh

I am a common man who misplaces his car keys, looks for his spectacles when they are perched on his forehead, and enjoys singing a golden oldie in the company of friends. *A common man who achieved meaningful success by setting powerful multidimensional and balanced goals and paved the path to them with determination.*

It's not uncommon for people to achieve phenomenal professional success, only to find that they are mysteriously disappointed and unhappy. This empty feeling has been reported in several studies by seemingly successful people, including CEOs, government leaders, scientists, athletes, entertainers and award-winners in every walk of life. In a study of CEOs of Fortune 500 companies at Yale University, many apparently highly successful professionals reported that they felt their lives were incomplete and disappointing at many levels.

Professor C. Clayton of Harvard University, author of *The Innovator's Dilemma*, talks about an intriguing phenomenon. He did a study of his MBA students at Harvard. At their fifth-year reunion, they were doing fairly well; they had great spouses, jobs, houses and cars. At the tenth reunion, many had achieved professional success, but one-third reported being unhappy in life. At the twenty-fifth reunion, the situation was even bleaker. Although most people were doing well at work and financially, many had been unhappy, divorced or were grappling with relationship issues. Some had serious health issues, and some had even ended up in jail for unethical business practices.

What had gone wrong with these smart people after such a terrific start?

The answer is simple and lies buried in the nature of the goals. Possibly, they pursued single-dimensional success by chasing money or only professional success, and in doing so, sacrificed other things that were important for achieving meaningful success.

As observed by Prof. Clayton, many professionally successful people focus too much on becoming the person they want to be at work and far too little on the person they want to be holistically. Investing our time and energy in raising wonderful children or deepening the relationship with your spouse, parents, family and friends often doesn't show any clear evidence of return for many years.

Andrew Carnegie sums it up neatly: 'If you want to be happy, set goals that command your thoughts, liberate your energy, and inspire your hopes.' And he did!

Carnegie, who started his career as a bobbin boy at a cotton factory earning $1.20 a week, went on to sell his company, Carnegie Steel, for around $480 million, making him one of the world's richest men!

After selling his steel company, this petite-framed colossus, just five feet, three inches tall, retired from business and devoted himself full-time to philanthropy.

He gave away some $350 million (the equivalent of billions in today's dollars); really the bulk of his wealth. Among his philanthropic activities, he funded the establishment of more than 2500 public libraries around the globe, donated more than 7600 organs to churches worldwide and endowed organizations dedicated to research in science, education, world peace and other causes. Among his gifts was the $1.1 million for the land and construction costs of Carnegie Hall, the New York City concert venue that opened in 1891. He also funded the Carnegie Institution for Science, Carnegie Mellon University and the Carnegie Foundation. A lover of books, he was the largest individual investor in public libraries in American history.

Carnegie's mother, who was a major influence on his life, lived with him until her death in 1886. I view this similarity wistfully since my mother, too, was a major influence on my life, teaching me the importance of pursuing the right goals.

I often say that if you do not make decisions about your life, someone else will. People without goals end up working for people *with* goals! So, it is important that you are goal-driven and set your own goals.

Once you've set your goals, create a strategy and plan and **write it down** along with milestones. According to many studies, people with *written* goals have an 80 per cent higher probability of achieving them. I am one of these people.

To me, success wasn't something I would gauge by comparing against *others*. I strived to compete with myself after defining what meaningful success meant to me. If success to you means becoming a cricketer, singer or painter, go for it. But strive to be the best that your potential holds. It is also important to be *joyful and positive* while you are pursuing your goals and going through your life's journey. According to research in positive psychology, happy, positive and joyful people have a higher probability of achieving their goals and success.

Another thing about goals that I learnt and applied was that goals need to be *well-rounded*. **Multidimensional goals keep the wheel of life balanced and help you achieve meaningful success**, consequently creating a deeply satisfying, happy and fulfilling life.

What if you have the option to design your life the way you want and become the person you aspire to be? What goals will you have to achieve to reach that ideal state and lead a meaningful and joyful life? How do you create these goals? These are the questions you need to answer before embarking on the journey to meaningful success. Most people design their life around their career. There is nothing wrong with it, but a better way might be that you design your ideal life and define your long-term life goals first, then figure out the career goals within that framework. Whatever works best for you! Take the example of Sridhar Vembu, the founder of Zoho Corporation. He wanted to make a positive impact on smaller cities and villages by creating jobs and economic development there while keeping his professional aspirations of creating a global technology product company intact. The result, after twenty-five years of work, is that not only has he created a globally successful product and a multibillion-dollar company, but also a massive number of jobs in smaller cities. So, *take time to figure out the way you wish to design your life*. I promise that you will look back on it as the most important thing you would have ever done.

I have defined my wheel of goals in eight areas of life, as shown in Fig. 1. These eight areas are important to me. Similarly, each one of you has to decide your own life goals based on what is important to you. Goals will change at different stages in life. But the important thing is to have well-defined and well-rounded life goals when taking a long-term view. Depending on what stage of life you are in, you can focus on a select few, say five. However, the key is to make sure that *in the long term, you achieve all the goals you set for yourself.* This will help you achieve meaningful success that will give you true, fulfilling and lasting happiness! These goals can be created at any age and stage of your life.

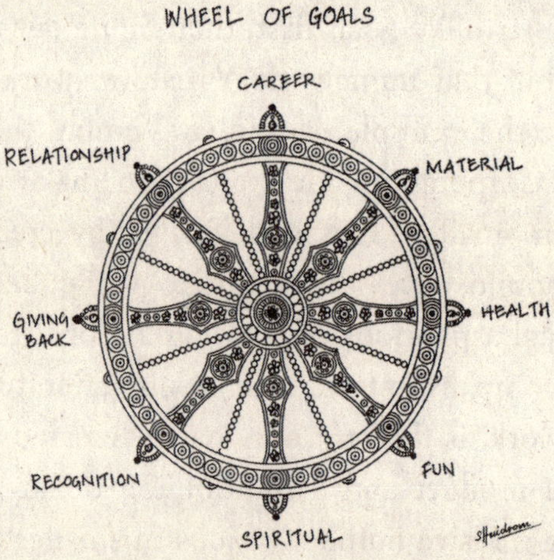

WHEEL OF GOALS

Fig. 1: My Wheel of Goals

Life goals, as shared in Fig. 1, can be largely divided into two groups, professional goals and well-being goals.

My professional goals comprised career (including education), financial and material goals while well-being goals comprised relationship, health, fun, spiritual and giving back goals.

Setting Professional Goals

When setting your professional goals, be aspirational, think big and do not worry about the constraints that you may face while achieving them.

Shoot for the stars because even if you miss, you will land on the moon. If you have a hard time freeing yourself from constrained thinking, assume that if god grants you three wishes for your personal and professional aspirations, what would you ask for? These are the goals you might want to set for yourself.

> 'The greater danger for most of us is not that our aim is too high and we miss it, but that it is too low and we reach it.'
>
> —Michelangelo

Once the goals are set, become obsessed with them and go after them passionately. To achieve these seemingly difficult goals, you must become *the best version of yourself and the person who deserves to attain these goals*. Improve skills in your core function, build leadership skills, pursue excellence and train yourself to think outside the box to get there.

Let me give you a simple example: If you set a goal to run 100 metres in 12 seconds, it may look impossible from where you are today. An average man can run 100 metres in 27 seconds while a woman can run 100 metres in 34 seconds. An average athlete can run 100 metres in 14 seconds. But, if you train like Usain Bolt (9.58 sec) or Florence G. Joyner (10.49 sec), the Olympic champions, is it possible for you to reach at least 12 seconds? Yes, it is absolutely possible!

When Farhan Akhtar, a Bollywood actor who was not an athlete, started preparing to play Milkha Singh (the Flying Sikh, an Indian track and field sprinter) on screen in the movie *Bhaag Milkha Bhaag*, he began training with astounding zeal. And he was running 100 metres in less than 12 seconds when the movie was ready to be shot!

This is the power of that one decision you take, to become the best version of yourself. I strongly believe, if your goal is to be a CEO or to own a $100 million company, *no one can stop you as long as you are willing to work passionately and become the person who deserves it*. So, set big goals and become worthy of achieving these goals.

> '*Everything comes to us that belongs to us if we create the capacity to receive it.*'
>
> —Rabindranath Tagore

Do not forget to find yourself a mentor and become a good mentee. Also, draw inspiration from people whom you admire and who can be your role models. Chapters 3 to 8 will guide you through this journey.

Setting Well-being Goals

If life were a coin, professional goals would be on one side and well-being goals on the other. Well-being goals are as important as professional goals. *Relationships are your most valuable assets; spirituality is the rock for your soul; health, the base from which any other achievement can be pursued; and giving back, the deep replenishment for your inner self.* When one is caught up in chasing professional success, these well-being goals often slip down in priority. The only way to ensure they don't slip is to be as rigorous in setting these goals as you are in setting professional goals. These well-being goals provide you with a platform and make you a person ready to achieve your professional goals. Chapters 9 to 11 will throw light on how to make this happen.

How much *time and effort* should one devote to each goal category? Here is a suggestion, as shown in Fig. 2, but ultimately you decide for yourself. Of course, the weighting will change based on your goals and stage of life.

Professional Goals: Career/Education/Financial/ Material Goals—70 per cent

Well-being Goals: Relationship Goals—15 per cent, Health/Sports/Fun Goals—10 per cent, Spiritual/ Giving Back Goals—5 per cent

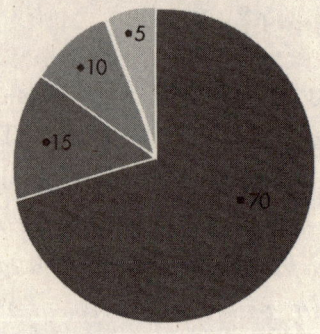

■ Career/Education/Financial/Material Goals
● Relationship Goals
◆ Health/Sports/Fun Goals
● Spiritual/Giving Back Goals

Fig. 2: Typical weighting of various goals in percentage

Another important piece of advice: You will be able to achieve goals only if you are committed to articulating and writing them down as SMART goals. SMART is an acronym for Specific, Measurable, Achievable, Realistic and Timely. Therefore, a SMART goal incorporates all of these criteria to help focus your efforts and increase the chances of achieving your goal. This is an age-old but very reliable and handy method.

Let me explain this process by creating a lifetime wheel of goals for a student.

Example of Lifetime Wheel of Goals for a Student

These lifetime goals can be set at any point in time. However, the earlier, the better! Doing this exercise will give you long-term clarity on what you wish to achieve in your life. Conceptualize a clear vision of your end state, think big, challenge yourself and aim to be the best version of yourself while doing this activity. Write these goals down and keep referring to them. Always keep them in your diary/laptop and mind space. Of course, these are your goals and will change as per your aspirations and life situations, but still, it is a great start.

Long-term Lifetime Goals for a Student:

- Education Goals: Do an MBA programme, law, engineering, finance or medicine degree from a good university.
- Career Goals: Be a CXO, or an owner of a Rs 100-crore business or practice, or the most-sought-after heart surgeon in the city or establish an NGO to impact an area of my choice.
- Financial Goals: Reach a net worth of Rs 1 or 10 or 100 crore in my lifetime.
- Material Goals: Own a house/apartment and a specific car.
- Health Goals: Maintain an optimal and balanced body mass index (BMI), keep lifestyle-related diseases away.
- Relationship Goals: Get married by the age of thirty, have a kid by thirty-five, spend two hours a day with family as family time, mentor kids, be best friends with my spouse, support and spend quality time with parents, extended family and friends.

- Spiritual Goals: Have a meaningful relationship with the Almighty, a mind and body connection, and inner peace. Achieve this by choice of mind-calming regimens like prayer or meditation on a disciplined schedule.
- Giving Back Goals: Educate ten or 100 lesser privileged children, extend medical care to 100 less fortunate people, donate Rs 10 lakh to a charity, give back through a Rotary Club or an NGO.
- Fun Goals: Visit ten countries, learn Hindustani classical music or kathak dance, and get your golf handicap under twelve.

See, it wasn't that difficult, was it? It's just about having the discipline to take time out and think about what you want to achieve in your lifetime. ***Explore yourself deeply and think about things that matter to you***. Most importantly, don't miss any category that is important to you.

Once you have long-term goals laid out neatly, it's time to break them down into shorter-term goals along with timelines.

If you are new to setting goals—I believe some of you would be—and you are unable to think of long-term life goals, you can also start by creating your five/ten/fifteen-year goals. Although it is better to start with long-term life goals, shorter-term life goals, of around five/ten years, should help you move in the direction of your long-term life goals.

Let me explain by creating a wheel of goals via this sample of ten-to-fifteen-year goals for a thirty-year-old professional (several more examples are shared in the appendix):

Example of Ten-to-Fifteen-year Goals for a Thirty-year-old Professional

- Career Goals: Become a director/VP in the next ten years. Focus on getting the right experiences to be ready for this career progression. Develop personal excellence, out-of-the-box thinking and leadership skills as you progress along this path. Make short-term goals based on milestones that will help you build these critical success skills. Achieve excellence in your job, take on difficult projects, and come up with new ideas to solve customer problems.
- Educational Goals: Complete your education from a good institution. Read twenty books in your field of interest to keep up to date and continue to learn. Identify people who inspire you and your role models, read their work and learn from them as much as possible. Find a mentor and have regular sessions.
- Financial Goals: Have a net worth of Rs 1 or 5 or 10 crore. Begin to support parents/other family (as required). Begin saving and investing with clear goals.
- Material Goals: Buy a car/apartment. Get membership to an athletic or golf club.

- Health Goals: Exercise every day for forty-five minutes using any method of choice. Team sports, like basketball after work, help to build relationships while providing you a good workout!
- Relationship Goals: Get married, start a family and spend quality time with your spouse, children, parents and extended family. Build a strong group of genuine friends and a professional network.
- Spiritual Goals: Meditation and/or prayer, fifteen–thirty minutes per day.
- Fun Goals: Go on vacation every year for seven days with family and/or friends. Start a terrace garden. Learn a new craft. Watch a movie every week.
- Giving Back Goals: Volunteer/donate to charity, sponsor the education of three less privileged kids, extend medical care to ten less fortunate people—whatever suits you.

Once you have written down your goals, as shown in the sample, break down each goal into multiple milestones. *At any point in life, you should have clear five-year goals.* Create a strategy around these goals, make a plan and start right away.

Let's take Maya's example. She is passionate about saving lives through medical technology and has set a career goal of reaching the vice president position at a large medical technology company in fifteen years. She needs to break it down. In ten years, she has to become a director; in five, a senior manager; in two, a manager; and in one year, she must deliver superlative performance in her current role and work hard on building leadership and other skills. At every level, she needs to *identify the skills and experience she needs to get to the next level*, and she must learn these skills while getting the right experiences. As you can see from this example, breaking big goals down into smaller, more manageable goals makes it far clearer how the goals will be accomplished. ***Achieving smaller goals first is the best way for you to develop confidence and self-belief.*** The key for Maya is to become the person who is ready for the position of vice president in fifteen years.

Setting Career Goals

Setting career goals can be challenging. As shown in Fig. 3 overleaf, *your career 'sweet spot' lies in the intersection of the areas you are interested in, the areas you are talented at, the areas that the world values and the areas that allow you to achieve your other life goals.* Hence, look for a career that really excites you, is packed with growth and learning opportunities and lets you plan and have an overall fulfilling life.

As an example, let us say you like and are good at Artificial Intelligence (AI). The world needs this skill, too, and you feel that Google in the US would be the right place for you to realize your potential. However,

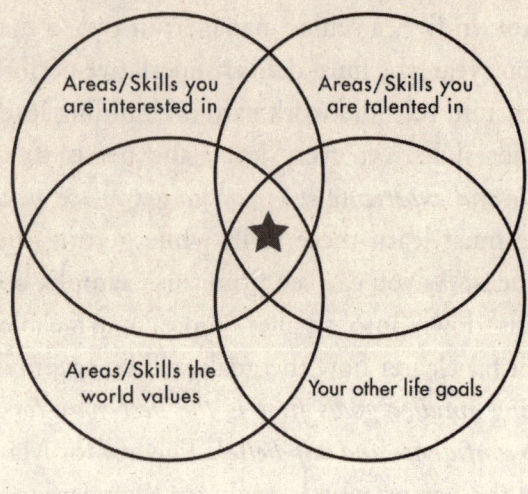

★ *Your Career Sweet Spot*

Fig. 3: Career sweet spot

your other life goals, family, health (say ayurvedic treatment), art (say kathak dance) or giving back, require you to be in India. In that case, a good solution may be to work at Google or for some other company in India in the area of AI.

It is important to understand that you will rarely get a job that you will like 100 per cent. There will be some parts that you will enjoy and some that you won't. Most people will do well in the parts that they like but keep cursing the part they do not like. However, I have seen that people who do well in the long run are the ones *who do well in what they like and who also do well in what they do not like*. They cannot be great cricketers if they are great at batting or bowling but poor at fielding; it does not matter whether they like fielding or not. If they drop a few catches regularly, they are done. Rahul Dravid was a phenomenal batsman and a great fielder, but many times he did wicket-keeping; it didn't matter whether he liked it or not. It was needed for the team. So, the focus should be on getting a job that you mostly like, moves you closer to your career goals and gives you an opportunity to learn. It may not be a perfect job, as that may not even exist.

> *'Love what you do until you find something you will love to do.'*
>
> —Dr Vivek Mansingh

Setting Career Goals in High School

You should set your first goals when you are in the ninth or tenth grade. It may look difficult, but it really isn't if you keep it simple and think hard. Timing is important because you may have to start choosing subjects that take you in a particular career direction. Here are some tips for high school students in setting their career goals.

Most likely, this is the first time you are setting goals, but do not feel intimidated. Keep it simple and just get started.

Look for a profession that excites you; it is better if it is aligned to the subjects that you like and are good at.

Your early role models, such as parents, uncles, aunts or friends' parents, may give you a clue about the profession you may be excited about.

You can also look at people whom you admire and see if you want to follow in their footsteps.

You may also want to take an aptitude test to evaluate your strengths and the careers that would suit you best.

The biggest dilemma at this stage is that you may not be able to differentiate between a hobby and a career. Look at the successful people in your choice of career and see if you would like a life like theirs.

If you like cricket and want to choose it as a career, please ensure that a knowledgeable person evaluates you to see if you do indeed have the core skills. Learn from coaches and successful cricketers the pluses and minuses of being a cricketer, and also learn what it would take to become a successful cricketer in terms of fitness, training and hard work. Take stock of the risks, too. Sometimes, these choices are difficult, so ask for help from a mentor, a person who can guide you.

Your choice of career 'sweet spot' at this stage lies at the intersection of careers you are interested in and areas you are talented at.

So, if you do not like biological sciences, do not pick a medical career just because it is financially rewarding or because your parents are doctors.

Figure out your study plan based on your choice of career and work hard to get into the best college possible.

Getting into your college of choice will be your short-term goal.

What if you still do not have this clarity? Move ahead with your core strength: the subjects you like. Do your best and keep learning about the possible career choices, and the path will become clearer in due course.

I chose engineering as it always fascinated me right from childhood. My sons, Anant and Ayush, chose careers in finance in high school and built their college and career strategy around it. With some hard thinking, guidance and following the steps mentioned above, you will be able to define your career goals. It will not be cast in stone, so don't freeze; take the best shot with the information you have. It is better to have a goal in front of you than no goal because you can't decide at this stage.

Setting Career Goals When Ready for Your First Job

Look for challenging work, recognition, responsibility and growth, not just salary.

Choose a career that you feel passionately about, even if it is not as financially rewarding at the beginning.

Remember, if you have a successful career, you will earn more in the last ten years of your career than in the first thirty. Your chances of doing well are much better if you have passion for your work. So, follow your passion, then develop the skills and experience needed for long-term success.

Actively spot the areas of work that you love; which will give you a clue as to which direction you should take your career.

What if you do not have this clarity? Take the best path available to you that is in line with your core strengths. However, keep looking for a career path that excites you while developing the skills needed to become a well-rounded professional.

Don't allocate all your resources only to goals that provide tangible results, such as career growth. Instead, create a balance among all the goals that are important to you.

If ever in your career you have to compromise your values, walk away.

The Power of Setting Goals

Quite early in my professional life, other than setting my career goals, I set the goal of achieving financial independence by the age of forty. I wasn't driven by greed for wealth but by a crystal-clear vision of freedom: freedom from working to meet material needs, so that I could focus on other goals by the time I blew out forty candles on my birthday cake. As mentioned earlier, I did achieve my goal by inventing an instrument. If I had not set this aspirational goal, I would never have achieved it. That is the power of setting goals.

'Imagination is everything. It is a preview of life's coming attractions.'

—Albert Einstein

This strikes a chord for me! One needs to release the mind like an ocean releases its waves—free, unhampered, unimpeded. Let your imagination run wild like a child on a playground. Visualize the end state of your successful journey that is exciting and you feel passionate about. The end state should get etched in your subconscious mind, leaving deep markings on it. *Creating a vision board with your end state and goals in pictures is a sure way of keeping them at the top of your mind.* Pictures of people who inspire you, relationships you would like to develop, the type of house and car you want to own, the job you would be excited about, the places you would like to travel to, all of these can be put on your vision board.

'I visualized where I wanted to be, what kind of player I wanted to become, and I focused on getting there,' said Michael Jordan, arguably the greatest basketball player in American history.

Managing Your Wheel of Goals

You don't have to give an equal amount of time and focus to every goal every day, but you need to find a place for every goal over a long period of time. Before my first entrepreneurial foray in the US, I talked to my wife and kids and told them that they would see much less of me for the next eighteen months. They lent me their precious support. It was tough but I had to put relationships and other goals on the back burner for that period.

You may want to focus on your top five goals every year; however, make sure by rotation you are able to focus on all your goals over your lifetime.

A good balance means spending the RIGHT amount of time and focus on each of your goals based on priority, not EQUAL amounts of time and focus on each goal.

As you live your life day to day, you need to make sure that you are cognizant of the time and effort you are allotting to your prioritized goals. A balanced goal wheel is of no use unless you give the right amount of time and focus to your prioritized goals.

Make sure that only professional goals do not get all your focus while well-being goals get ignored.

When you decide your long-term goals, think long and hard about how you would like to be remembered at the end game. This will energize you and also clarify any conundrums in your mind.

It is important to remember:

'Your future should not be decided by an extrapolation of your past. It should be driven by the aspirations of the future.'

—Dr Vivek Mansingh

Once you understand that goal-setting is the first step to achieving meaningful success, you will constantly think about goals like a lover obsessed with their loved one! If you find yourself doing that, you are on the right track.

Setbacks Are a Part of Life

I also learnt to take setbacks in stride. As a young man ready for college, I faced my first blow. The paper IIT entrance exam was in English! Drops of sweat formed on my forehead: having been a Hindi-medium student, most of the questions were difficult to comprehend. Predictably, it didn't go very well. So, instead of an IIT, I got a seat at the National Institute of Technology (NIT) Allahabad.

contd.

But I had imbibed an important lesson quite early: do not complain! I had studied at the Government Inter College in Fatehpur with classmates who didn't have proper clothes or even electricity in the house.

But to make up, I set myself the goal to graduate at the top of the class at NIT, and I did.

One of my start-ups, Jasmine Networks, ran out of money during the financial meltdown in 2000. I lost my job at the peak of the recession and just after I moved to India.

I had built the hardware design team at Dell India by putting my heart and soul into it. But even after successfully designing several servers, we had to move the hardware design to Dell Taiwan and I had to dismantle the whole team.

A few start-ups I have incubated have failed for various good and bad reasons.

Such challenges come in everyone's life, even if you are talented, work hard and do everything by the book.

There are many more such failures I have faced, but one must remain positive, persevere, learn from these experiences and move on.

Remember, failure is not the opposite of success, it is a springboard to success.

'You will face many defeats in life, but never let yourself be defeated.'—Maya Angelou

You will encounter challenges; goals related to career and finances will appear tangible and get the time, effort and focus, while well-being goals will be hard to measure and get ignored. Question yourself hard; trust me, the answers are inside you, not out there in the world. Listen to your heart and you will hear them just as Ric did.

Imagine that just after your plane has just taken off, there is a loud noise and the plane starts shuddering. This is what happened to Ric. He was on US Airways flight 1549 that landed in the Hudson River, and fortunately all passengers survived. As people screamed, a searing clarity filled his mind. *Why hadn't he lived more in the moment? Why hadn't he been there for the people he loved, especially his family, spouse, kids? Why hadn't he mended more fences? Had he been wasting the unique opportunity called* life *that he had been given?* From that day onwards, Ric's life changed. He sliced the pie of his goals differently and led a more balanced and meaningful life. Why wait for a life-changing event like a near-fatal plane crash to slice your goal pie differently? Do it now! I am glad I could focus on all parts of my goal-wheel.

At this point in life, I inspect myself: *Am I the human being I'd want my children to be? Am I a good role model for my children, nieces and nephews?* These two questions are the best litmus tests.

My balanced goal wheel is an open book for everyone to peek in. My professional/intellectual goals of becoming one of the best in my field became a reality through my designs, patents, books and technical papers.

My financial, material and fun goals have been achieved in a well-oiled manner. I was able to travel to more than fifty countries. I am particularly fascinated by wildlife and have been lucky to visit wildlife parks in India, Africa and the US. I am sticking to my goal of reading at least twenty books per year.

Relationship goals have always remained as clear as the taste of my mother's kababs in my head! I worked hard to do my best for my parents, wife, sons, immediate and extended family and friends. Today, I enjoy mentoring my sons, daughter-in-law, nieces and nephews and hundreds of others with whom I have cultivated meaningful relationships over the years.

My awards—Who's Who of USA and IT Man of the Year, India—bear testimony to my earning recognition goals.

In recent years, I may have sporadically been tardy but overall, fitness and health have always been goals I never let go of. I try to eat right and work out; the occasional bowl of butter chicken throwing me off target, I must confess.

Moving on to spiritual goals, I'd like to emphasize that these goals cannot be put away for 'when I have the time'. Make time for faith and you will reap its benefits. My faith guides me to prayers and studying our scriptures. I have undertaken courses offered by Yoganandji, Sri Sri Ravi Shankar and Sri Sadhguru Ji. Discipline around these goals has given me courage and fortitude during difficult times. I also feel that whatever I could achieve is a reward emanating from my untiring faith.

Finally, the goal of giving back to society is written, quantified by me on my yearly goalsheet. I follow up on those without fail. Given this rigour, I have been able to uplift thousands in Fatehpur, my hometown, through several programmes. Now I would like to 'Mentor A Million' young people with this book at the core.

As I inspect my life in the rearview mirror, I feel grateful that I didn't just plunge into a gushing river of opportunities and let the gush take me wherever. Instead, I stepped on stones that were carefully placed goals and charted my own course. The river meandered through all sorts of terrain; sometimes it was serene and at other times, it swirled with force. But my goals kept me on track.

Every year, when people hang their stockings for Santa Claus and put up their Christmas trees, I make use of the holidays to write my goals for the coming year and do a self-evaluation of the previous year's goals that I had set for myself. *I try to be my own Santa, my gifts being the goals I'd go on to achieve! Trust me, it is a very powerful exercise.*

'You are what your deep desire is.
As your desire is, so is your will.
As your will is, so is your deed.
As your deed is, so is your destiny.'

—The Upanishads

Key Learnings

1. Success comes from deciding what you want to achieve and working passionately towards achieving it.
2. Define what meaningful success is to you and elucidate it as goals covering all aspects of life.
3. These goals can be created at any age and stage of your life.
4. Write these goals down and review them and your progress as frequently as possible.
5. You don't have to give equal amounts of time and focus to *every* goal of yours *every* single day and at *every* stage of your life, but you need to find a place for every goal that is meaningful to you over a period of time.
6. Visualize the end state; how it would all be once you have achieved all your goals.
7. Passionately work on all your goals and become the best version of yourself by improving your professional and personal skills as discussed in this book.

Guru Mantra on the Power of Goals:
Kiran Mazumdar-Shaw, founder, Biocon

I was driven by the goal of wanting to put India on the world map of biotechnology research and development of medicines. I felt very proud when India started to get noticed in this area. I also had a goal to put Biocon on the map of the world as it relates to diabetes, cancer and autoimmune disease medicines. Slowly, we are getting there. Such goals drive me!

Mentee Speaks on the Power of Goals:
Sujay Datta, vice president, Evalueserve

Among the many lessons that I have received from Dr Vivek's mentorship, the two key ones are:

Learning to aim higher and aspiring for more in both personal and professional life. My success criteria have changed and are pegged much higher today than what they were a few years back. Now I have the confidence to walk for many more miles; something that, at one point in time, I didn't believe I was capable of.

I have also learnt to be goal-driven. I now break my long-term career goals into short-term, plausible milestones. I plan and execute in meaningful steps, without losing clarity of the long-term vision. This simple exercise has made progress in life a doable reality.

BECOME THE BEST
VERSION OF YOURSELF

DREAMS

ASPIRATIONS

THE WHOLE UNIVERSE SUPPORTS YOUR PASSION

THREE

Passion: The Miracle Ingredient

'*Nothing great in the world has been accomplished without passion.*'

—Georg Hegel

'*Main Amitabh Bachchan bol raha hoon, Akashwani se . . .*'

The story of a young Amitabh auditioning at All India Radio (AIR) for the job of radio announcer and getting rejected is the starting point of a tale of passion and persistence through failures. Several unsuccessful movie role auditions followed, but he didn't give up. He passionately followed his dream in acting and overcame a life-threatening accident to become a megastar that none have come even close to.

I have had the good fortune of working with many successful and accomplished people around the world, and *they all have one thing in common: passion*. These people eat, drink and think about the challenge at hand; they keep asking, what more can I do to achieve my goals; they are completely obsessed with it.

I can relate to this sentiment so well. In my life's journey, I have discovered that passion is the vital force that powers the hard work, determination, creativity and perseverance needed to achieve goals amid the impediments that come (I must add that they come in generous measure!) in one's path. I get this big rumbling, flammable wave inside, firing up my soul whenever I embark on achieving any of my goals.

The Magic of Passion

It was a warm summer morning in Fatehpur when I reached home after a four-hour bus journey, my graduate degree and gold medal in my dusty satchel, to announce to my parents, 'I will go abroad for my postgraduate studies.' In those pre-Internet days, I hadn't the faintest idea how I would go about it. Or how I would fund it.

The lack of resources never deterred me. I would announce my goal, however larger than life it was, and then passionately throw myself into achieving it. The magic of passion is that you get some amazing ideas to achieve your seemingly

contd.

impossible goals. Instead of applying to the office of admissions of US/Canada universities, I wrote to several professors whose area of research appealed to me.

One of those was Prof. Oosthuizen at Queen's University, Canada, who worked in the area of computational fluid mechanics. After seeing my passion and preparation, he got me a full scholarship to enable my MS and PhD studies.

One cannot be passionate without goals and aspirations. *So, the first step is setting clear goals*—that's the step that illuminates the puzzling path ahead. Then, if you have an earnest desire and obsession for your goals, passion follows and does its magic.

Here is how passion delivers the goods. The human brain has two parts: one that works through logic, and the second, the more powerful part, that works through emotions. Most of the time, we are working through the logical part of the brain. However, if we can also engage the other, emotional part of the brain, and both start working in tandem, we can generate amazing power and become a superhuman being to achieve seemingly impossible goals. But, as mentioned earlier, one needs emotion, not logic, to engage the emotional part of the brain. ***That emotion is passion***.

Let me prove that the emotional part of the brain is much more powerful. Ever cried while watching a movie even while knowing it was fiction? You know very well that it is not real, but once emotions have charged the more powerful emotional part of the brain, the logical part of the brain cannot control you, and you cry.

I remember watching the movie *Taare Zameen Par*, a Hindi movie that tracks the journey of an eight-year-old dyslexic child. Tears clouded my eyes as I watched the innocent child grapple with his father's rejection and problems at the hostel he is packed off to. I knew it was fiction, I knew that it was a movie but still, my emotions charged the more powerful part of my brain and it got the better of my logical part. Don't tell me it has never happened to you!

So, for the goals you are truly passionate about, once ***both the logical and the emotional parts of the brain start working together, the whole universe conspires to help you achieve your goals***. *Aham Brahmasmi* at work.

Let me explain: Aham Brahmasmi is a term that is used in Hindu philosophy to describe the unity of the *atman* (individual self or soul) with *brahman* (the creator).

The term comes from the Sanskrit, *aham*, meaning 'I', and *brahma*, meaning 'divine' or 'sacred'. While Brahma is the Hindu creator god, *asmi* translates to 'I am'. You will experience the universe, the *brahmand* or *kayanat* around you pouring in its support in surprising and mysterious ways to carry you towards your goal. Let's say that you desperately and passionately wanted to meet Ratan Tata; well, he might come and sit next to you on a flight. That is the power of the whole universe helping you.

Try it yourself—charge the emotional centre of your brain through passion and align it to your goals. It will feel like a dam has been demolished and released an outpouring of energy. And once your whole brain gets charged, the universe will conspire to help you fulfil your goals.

Passion sprinkled with self-belief creates an enormous force to help you ride through the obstacles that come in your way. Self-belief is having confidence in your own abilities and believing you can do anything you set your mind to. Healthy self-belief gives you strength to face failure without you feeling diminished as a person. According to Ford, your belief in yourself is a determining factor in your success.

> *'If you think you can do a thing or think you can't do a thing, you're right.'*
>
> —Henry Ford

The innovation dreams I pursued and the resulting inventions were born purely out of passion and self-belief. Once I had set myself a significant material goal of financial independence, a tough road lay ahead. I had no idea how to achieve my goal but passion showed the way. I figured out that the most practical way for me to achieve this goal was through invention. But, invent what? What would be useful and unique? In addition to the sleepless nights, I spent hours researching at the libraries of Stanford and working in my garage. But the end result was a globally successful instrument invention achieved purely through the power of passion.

The same holds true for goals related to careers. If you have identified a career that you are passionate about, go for it, even if the beginning stages are not as attractive and the future is uncertain. My son Ayush gave up a Google US job to take a job at an impact investing firm, Social Finance, in San Francisco, at a much lower compensation, because he is passionate about impact investing.

What if you are one of those who isn't sure about which career or job you are passionate about? Then work towards a career that is aligned with your strengths. Pick a job that leverages your skills, competencies and inclination. Then, strive to give it your best and be passionate about what you do. As I mentioned earlier, there is no job where you will like everything you have to do. There will be some parts of the job that you will like and some you will not. However, I always say that people who do well in both, the parts they like and the parts they do not like, do extremely well in their careers. Multiple studies show that 90 per cent of employees are not happy with their job. Hence, they keep complaining about their jobs. What they do not realize is that it hurts them most. How about deciding not to complain and doing whatever you have to do with full sincerity and passion? Keep learning and developing your skills in whatever you do. This small, positive change will work wonders.

By remaining so, over time, you will build a great brand and discover which part of the job you love and are passionate about. Then work on finding a field and a job where you can maximize the parts of the job you love.

Steve Jobs said, 'The only way to be truly satisfied is to do what you believe is great work. And the only way to do great work is to love what you do. If you haven't found it yet, keep looking. Don't settle. As with all matters of the heart, you'll know when you find it.'

Be a hungry search engine and keep your antenna up, I'd add.

A good example of passion-driven people are the founders of start-ups. They find a problem or an area they are passionate about and then throw themselves in, fully understanding the challenges they face. Most founders I have worked with leave secure well-paid jobs to launch their start-ups in spite of uncertainties and pressures, but it is passion that drives them.

In my life's journey, passion hustled me on and helped me jump over hurdles. It changed the glasses I wore. Through these new glasses, I viewed adversity as an exciting opponent to beat. Whether it was enrolling for a PhD without having the money for the fee, or the patents I registered, the start-ups I created or bagging the top jobs at Dell and Cisco, it was passion that took me places.

Currently, I am invested with a gripping passion to contribute to my country's start-up ecosystem through highly involved venture capital funding and mentoring. I leap out of bed each morning full of fervour to get on with a packed schedule. I also love to inspire people to achieve meaningful success in their lives through my talks and mentoring. Through this book and the associated website, I intend to help over one million people. Exciting, isn't it?

A colleague said, 'Vivek's passion is infectious.' Well, I'd love to infect millions with this wonderful virus called *passion*!

Key Learnings

1. Passion produces enthusiasm and excitement to achieve your goals.
2. All the successful people I have worked with closely, across fields and across geographies, have had one thing in common: passion.

3. If you have identified a career that you are passionate about, go for it, even if the beginning stages are not as appealing and the future appears uncertain.
4. True passion can change your orbit of success in whatever you are trying to achieve.

Guru Mantra on the Power of Passion from John Chambers, chairman and CEO, Cisco

I'm passionate about whatever I do. Even when I fail. It was my passion that helped me take Cisco from $1 billion in revenue to $47 billion during my tenure as CEO.

Mentee Speaks on the Power of Passion: Nayan Vaghela, director, Cisco

It was truly a pleasure for me to work with Dr Mansingh at Cisco. I still recall my first meeting with him about my career. He said, 'I have a magic trick to help you achieve anything you want, but you need to write down precisely what you want to achieve and by when.' It was a deceptively simple exercise—when I got down to it, I drew a blank on many fronts!

Thinking hard, I realized my passion was in product management. I translated my passion and dreams into goals supported by a strategy and implementation plan. He encouraged me to develop deep expertise and excellence in product management. 'Become the best product manager in your field,' he would say and show the path.

It has served me well. I have been promoted to the position of director of product management at Cisco. I am enjoying my job and am managing some of Cisco's global products. I have achieved much more professionally and personally. I am much more passionate about my goals now, which has given me a new energy and excitement towards life.

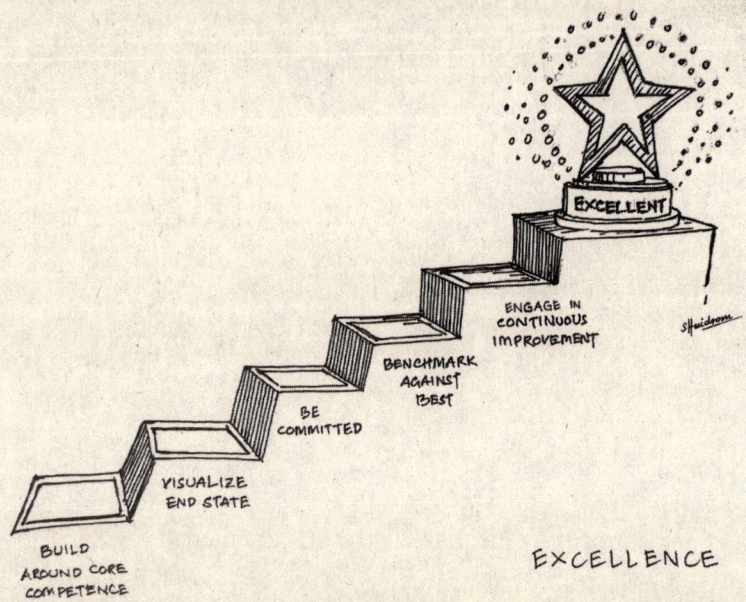

BUILD
AROUND CORE
COMPETENCE

VISUALIZE
END STATE

BE
COMMITTED

BENCHMARK
AGAINST
BEST

ENGAGE IN
CONTINUOUS
IMPROVEMENT

EXCELLENT

EXCELLENCE

FOUR

Excellence: Becoming the Best You Can Be

'The will to win, the desire to succeed, the urge to reach your full potential . . . these are the keys that will unlock the door to personal excellence.'

—Confucius

What is excellence? Simply put, it's the badge you get when you are outstanding in whatever you do. It's just top-notch. It's a consistent, repeatable output from you.

To identify who has achieved excellence in life, my general rule of thumb to apply is, *how do we know that person?* If they are not from within our known circle of family, friends and immediate co-workers, we know them because they have achieved a certain level of excellence in what they do: Rahul Dravid, Narayana Murthy, Amitabh Bachchan, to name a few.

Examples of excellence closer to you would be the person who topped your college, the go-to person on your team who is recognized for her deep understanding of the product, a leading surgeon or a lawyer and so on.

Five Prongs of Excellence

1. Excellence differentiates extraordinary people from ordinary people.
2. Most of us want excellence but are not ready to strive to achieve excellence.
3. Excellence starts with visualizing a very clear end state you wish to achieve, and passionately and relentlessly driving towards it.
4. Excellence means improving your performance consistently and continuously.
5. When you benchmark against other significant achievers, you improve and grow.

Why excellence? Each one of us may not have what it takes to become a Sachin Tendulkar or Ratan Tata, *but each one of us has to become the best we can be to realize the potential we have*. Excellence is the *not-so-secret* ingredient that is needed to become the best version of ourselves, to slash through whatever is inhibiting our best from blossoming. The result: becoming exceedingly good in our area of expertise, with the knowledge, skills and experience that are needed. What does excellence do? It builds a reputation and brand that sets you apart from the herd. If you like coding, become the best coder you possibly can. Define what it takes to become an excellent coder and do whatever it takes to get there. You may have to take a few classes, get exposure to certain kinds of projects, but there is no rocket science except relentlessly pushing yourself to get there. If you are a teacher or a doctor, become the best you can be. It makes you run your own race and opens up new paths to success.

> '*To achieve something that you have never achieved before, you must become someone that you have never been before.*'
>
> —Les Brown

A bunch of well-intentioned notions aren't enough; they have to be clear like the sparkling water of a mountain stream: the why, the how and the what of your specific goal of excellence have to be concrete! Would you like to get into the mind of a person who has achieved excellence? I had the good fortune of getting a peek into the mind of Rahul Dravid, one of the all-time bests in the game of cricket. He had a deep, burning desire to become simply the best in the game. Not to make money or become famous, just to become the best, period.

His goal was not just wishful thinking. It was reinforced with a solid strategy and an execution plan. The plan had the nuts and bolts of how to achieve his excellence goal—mastering techniques, relentless hard work, fitness training, mental toughness and so on.

The results of becoming one of the best in the world are fame, recognition and money. But these were not the drivers, these were the by-products. Like Rahul, I have seen many others reaching excellence over a period of time through *passionate desire, proper strategy, continuous improvement and relentless hard work*.

For the journey to excellence, one needs to know why, how and what. My 'why' was 'Excellence in engineering in my field and becoming the best in the world'. The 'how' was by championing technology and innovating with dogged determination. It took a ton of passion, continuous improvement and a will of steel. The 'what' was that I reached the number one spot in my field with innovative product designs like the iMac, my six patents, two books and scores of technical papers. Later, I decided to achieve excellence in the areas of public speaking and meeting my career goals of becoming a chairman, CEO, managing director; all of which I achieved through relentless hard work, continuous improvement and self-evaluation, and becoming the best I could be.

Seven Steps to Excellence

1. Have the hunger, know WHY you want to achieve the excellence you are striving for.

contd.

2. Be passionate about it.
3. Build excellence around your core competencies and capabilities.
4. Inculcate discipline and commitment.
5. Benchmark against the best.
6. Align your efforts with a solid strategy and plan.
7. Be engaged in constant self-evaluation and continuous improvement.

Have you heard about the 10,000-hour rule from the book *Outliers* by Malcolm Gladwell? It says that one has to work for 10,000 hours in an area to reach a certain level of excellence. Now, this amounts to working for seven years in that specific area (let's say you are working eight hours a day for 200 days per year). Here is the catch—you need to persist in that one area. If you get bored and wander away, your seven-year clock is reset. Excellence is generally about depth of knowledge and experience, not so much about breadth. But I know folks who are so passionate when chasing excellence that they end up working twenty-four hours a day. Yes, even while asleep, their minds are engaged and working. If they get up for a bio break, they practise a swing with an imaginary baseball or golf club. Such people complete 10,000 hours in 450 days instead of seven years! So, in three years they have accumulated fifteen years of experience and wisdom. We spot such examples in sports when a young Sachin Tendulkar hits the headlines or when a teenager becomes a grandmaster in chess or Neeraj Chopra wins an Olympic gold medal or an eighteen-year-old gets a PhD or my engineer gets the Michael Dell award for innovation. This is the result of passionate desire to achieve excellence.

> 'Perfection is not attainable; but if we chase perfection, we can catch excellence.'
>
> —Vince Lombardi

There aren't any shortcuts to excellence. Nor is the road lined with roses. The journey is as austere as a penance, as rigorous as an uphill trek and as humbling as a visit to an old-age home. But the rewards that await you at the end of it are supremely gratifying no matter where and what type of work you are doing.

Key Learnings

1. Each one of us has to become the best we can be to realize the potential we carry.
2. People develop excellence over a period of time through passionate desire, proper strategy, continuous improvement and relentless hard work.
3. Become outstanding in an area that you are passionate about by following the seven steps discussed in this chapter.
4. Each one of us may not become the best in the world, but by striving for excellence, we will become

the best version of ourselves and go much further in whatever we are trying to achieve.

Guru Mantra on Excellence: Rahul Dravid, 'The Wall' of cricket

To me, excellence is the constant effort to get the best out of myself. Excellence is a continuous journey. There are no rest stops. You have to keep evaluating your progress and improving.

Each one of us needs to realize our potential and become the best version of ourselves to do well in our careers and life. So, it is worth putting in your best efforts to pursue excellence.

Mentee Speaks on Excellence: Narayanan Subramaniam, senior director, Nutanix

It was the summer of 2009, and I was driving Dr Vivek back to his hotel after attending a team dinner in Austin that had been hosted by Dell. While waiting at a rather long traffic light, I said, 'Vivek, someday, I would like to be a prominent technology leader.'

Vivek paused in his characteristic style and then said something that had a profound impact on how I shaped my career.

'Narayanan, irrespective of whether you want to be a leader of technology at Dell or somewhere else, it's super important to have excellence and recognition in your field of technology and a personal brand around it.' It took me the better part of ten years to construct and execute what Vivek meant that evening, perhaps the best mentorship one-liner that I have had in my career. I developed deep expertise in some areas of technology by sheer hard work, determination and evaluating myself against other world-class technology leaders.

I've taken inspiration to create my own brand in the industry today and have become the best version of myself by following the path of excellence. I have achieved a lot more professionally and personally since then.

THINK
OUTSIDE THE BOX

FIVE

Think Outside the Box: Creativity and Innovation

'*Those who do not think outside the box are easily contained.*'

—Nicolas Manetta

Khadu walks with a swagger and digs out his trademark notepad and pencil when discussing a design. He is experienced and quite bright, and his work is impeccable. Khadu is my carpenter, and he has created some beautiful pieces of woodwork and furniture for our home. The only problem is that his experience has trained him to blurt out almost immediately, whenever presented with a tough ask, 'It can't be done, sir.' Not that he's entirely wrong—he speaks from experience that has taught him boundaries. Perhaps he has lost the ability to look at the problem differently. Or, *had* lost. Till he started working with me. I wouldn't let him tell me that it couldn't be done. Instead, I insisted, 'Tell me how it can be done differently to still reach the same objective!'

He had been schooled only till Grade 8, but he was quick to get the new way of working I was teaching him. He was quick to adapt—the naysayer changed into an innovative thinker quite effortlessly. Once he had done so, I challenged him further: I told him to give me two suggestions instead of one every time he came up with a solution.

As a result, the imposing staircase inside my house that once, according to him, wasn't possible, is not only there, it is there in a beautiful design made possible with a very quirky and different way of construction! How? Well, I can't share that—it's Khadu's intellectual property, in all fairness!

> *'Problems cannot be solved by thinking within the framework in which the problems were created.'*
>
> —Albert Einstein

One has to get creative to innovate. Creativity is that raw, ingenious, imaginative power of the brain to think differently while looking at the same problem. M.F. Hussain's paintings, Steve Jobs's products or Albert Einstein's theories are products of amazing creativity. **Innovation is the end-product or the child of creativity**.

Innovation is for Everyone

'*Don't pick the sound "no way" that is embedded in the word "Innovation"!*'

—Dr Vivek Mansingh

Innovation and creativity are not just for a few people in an organization; it is integral to all jobs. Every team member has to learn to think out of the box and come up with better ways of doing just about anything.

When innovation gets hands and legs and is implemented in the real world, it becomes an invention. In my experience, if you have trained yourself to be creative and work hard to use that creative energy to innovate at whatever job you can (it need not be patents, always!), you move closer to becoming the best version of yourself. You not only go a long way in your career but also get a great deal of intellectual satisfaction.

'*Innovation is a skill, a combination of art, science and creativity that can be learnt by individuals and companies.*'

—Dr Vivek Mansingh

Creativity is a process that needs no money and carries no risks. However, when we wish to transform creative ideas into innovation, a supportive organizational culture is critical.

Google's '20% Time' rule, which allows employees to innovate during work time, led to the invention of AdSense, Gmail and Google Talk (also known as Google Chat). 3M's similar allowance of 15 per cent of work time gave it the reputation of being an innovative workplace. Amazon has an interesting 'working backwards' process that encourages employees with a big idea to create a full dossier with a customer-impact statement, a mock press release, key questions and perspectives from different business areas. All of these are brilliant examples of organizations aiding innovation. Our own Tata's encourage and reward suggestions in a structured manner. Then there is the Johns Hopkins Applied Physics Laboratory that gives its people access to a state-of-the-art research complex that has led to close to 500 inventions! Sephora, the beauty company, organizes boot camps and mentoring for innovation. At both Cisco and Dell, I established a structured innovation programme encouraging and mentoring employees to take the seven steps of innovation (shown in the box) while providing organizational support to take the innovative ideas into reality.

Seven Steps to Innovation

1. Make innovation a quantified goal.
2. Examine the current solutions to the problem and challenge the status quo from all dimensions and in great detail.
3. Think out of the box and come up with multiple ideas.
4. You can also think about an ideal solution to the problem, without any constraints, and then converge to one strong and workable suggestion which brings you closest to the ideal solution.
5. Do not rest till you take the innovation to implementation.
6. Work with your company to file a patent if the solution is patentable.
7. Do not be afraid of collaboration with colleagues where needed.

'Innovation is 1 per cent inspiration and 99 per cent perspiration.'

—Thomas Edison

Coming to innovation at the individual level, you might think that only the brightest people of the world can innovate. This is a misconception. Firstly, there is no correlation between intelligence and creativity. Even a person with an average IQ score can be quite creative, with some variations. The belief that younger people are more creative isn't true, either. Research proves that we just 'forget' to use our creativity as we grow older.

So, how can you unleash your creativity and become innovative? It's really a habit, not a stroke of genius. It's just a skill to be worked at. It's the same as working hard to master riding a bike or learning to play an instrument.

> 'Imagination is the beginning of creation. You imagine what you desire, you will what you imagine, and at last, you create what you will.'
>
> —George Bernard Shaw

Set aside time to practise creativity. Do it religiously. Pick a problem and think about it. Allow yourself to daydream about it. You can visualize the exciting end-state of your solution. Then, work backwards to figure what you can and should do to get there!

Finally, fear is a deterrent that you need not be afraid of. If you are ready to fail, your propensity to be creative increases. Practice will make you more confident and reduce fear.

At Dell, when I challenged my team to come up with at least one innovative idea per person every year, there was some initial resistance. 'Where's the time to do all this?' 'We have never done it before and how can we do it, we are not even engineers,' some groaned. But, as I persisted, I witnessed a rich crop of the most amazing innovative ideas! *We made Dell India the most innovative Dell R&D site in Asia and were lauded by Michael Dell.* Not just the engineers—members of the documentation group too came up with some fantastic ideas.

Patents in India

Countries like the US and China file more than half a million patents in a year while India files less than 40,000 patents per year. Therefore, at this moment, we are far away from any of these leading countries on our innovation quotient. We as a country and individuals need to take up the innovation challenge with great sense of urgency.

My innovation moment came when I worked with Apple. The first product from Apple, after Steve Jobs came back as CEO the second time, was the iMac. Apple was in dire straits at that time. Steve asked the team to focus on a few select products instead of the thirty-odd that were being designed at that time. One of the top-priority products was the iMac. The challenge given by Steve was to design the iMac without any fan. A big challenge, given that the power dissipation by various components was high and the computer and monitor were combined into one. There were no comparable products that did not use a fan. However, we deeply analysed the problem, brainstormed on multiple innovative solutions, ran computer simulations and came up with an optimum solution which was later tested in the lab and then rolled out in the product. A remarkable feat which was admired by Steve Jobs himself when he launched the product at the Flint Centre in Cupertino with a lot of fanfare. Post that, my team and I received a personalized note of thanks, one of my prized possessions. A big poster of the iMac with a handwritten note that says, 'To Vivek and team, thank you so much for your help, we couldn't have done it without you.'

Passion for Innovation

I had hung up my boots post an immensely gratifying stint as president of the Collaboration & Communications Technology Group at Cisco India. A heart-warming farewell function was underway with many Cisco US leaders present, when a young girl raised her hand. In broken English, she asked:

'Why are you letting him leave? Under his leadership, I learnt how to innovate.' She was addressing Cisco US senior leaders and referring to a recent patent she had filed.

contd.

She sounded truly distraught. It wrenched my heart as much as it warmed it. She was a kindred spirit—a girl from a small town who was passionate about making her mark in Bangalore. I was glad I could stir up a passion for innovation in her.

Is there any difference between innovation in a large company versus that in start-ups? I'd say no: big or small, every company needs the power of innovation. When it comes to start-ups, there is always some innovation in the origin itself, considering its very existence has been sparked by the need for creative solutions to existing problems. Regardless of the nature of the start-up, innovation is necessary. It can be technology-based, business model-based, process-based or any other form. But there has to be some kind of innovation. Of course, in the case of start-ups, innovation is even more critical because it has to provide the start-up a sustainable and BIG competitive advantage. Start-ups need to take innovation seriously from the early stages, especially in their core areas, and file patents along the way.

I understand how a DNA for innovation can be incorporated into the culture of institutions. Currently, I am working towards making innovation a way of life in the start-ups I am working with. I hope to train minds to be fishing nets and dream catchers—always open wide and ready to catch ideas and translate them into inventions!

Remember, it is innovation that will take our companies and nation on a path of exponential economic growth!

Key Learnings

1. Innovation and creativity are not just for a few people inside an organization, they are integral to all.
2. Everyone should learn to think out of the box and come up with better ways of doing whatever they do.
3. One can learn and improve creativity and innovation by practising it, challenging oneself, and following the structured processes shared in this chapter.
4. Thinking out of the box can add a new dimension to your personal and professional life, can take you closer to becoming the best version of yourself and can bring all-round success closer.

Guru Mantra on Innovation: Narayana Murthy, founder, Infosys

I believe that innovation should not be the prerogative of a few seniors in the organization but it must be the mantra for everybody, from the janitor to the CEO. Only when innovation is owned by every employee in the company, and every employee asks this question, '*How do I do things faster, cheaper and better than yesterday?*' that an organization becomes strong.

Mentee Speaks on Innovation: Narayanan Subramaniam, senior director, Nutanix

In a one-on-one with Dr Vivek at Dell, we got talking about innovation and inevitably the topic of patents came up. 'Narayanan, how will you distinguish yourself from the many technology leaders in the industry?' he asked. Noticing my silence, he continued, 'Innovation, that's what you need to focus on, followed by patents. Patents show your creativity, your ability to innovate, and establish your expertise and excellence.'

The rest is history. I took the advice and guidance to heart and spent the next year churning out ideas on various topics ranging from IPv6 to security, resulting in several US patents. I became the first Dell employee in Asia to win the Michael Dell award for innovation and was recognized by Michael Dell at the annual Dell inventors' awards ceremony in 2008. Life and career have moved to a significantly positive trajectory since then.

LEADERSHIP
BECOMING 20 FEET TALL

SIX

Leadership: Becoming 20 Feet Tall

'Leadership starts where logic stops.'
—Dr Vivek Mansingh

'A leader is one who sees more than others see, who sees farther than others see, and who sees before others do,' said Leroy Eims. It made me curious: *How is it possible for one person to see farther than the rest?*

When Mahatma Gandhi along with our other freedom fighters embarked on a mission of getting freedom for India, all they had was passion, a strong vision and largely unorganized human resources, most of them poor and starving. Yet, the marvellous result: an independent India!

Their unwavering strength of character and their uncanny ability to see further than the rest went on to make them leaders the world still reckons by. To be able to visualize the future and forge on, a leader needs to be really tall. Like 20 feet, if we were to talk in literal terms. Well, no one is that tall! But one can be so by standing on the shoulders of another person! The biggest issue here is: *Why would anyone let you stand on their shoulders?* **The answer is simple: they will, if they like you, respect you, trust you and believe in your capability and the cause of the mission.** That sums up my view on leadership.

Dahi Handi, a hugely popular festival in Mumbai, involves communities hanging an earthen pot filled with dahi (yoghurt) or other milk-based delicacies at a height that is quite difficult to reach. Young men form teams and make a human pyramid to attempt to reach and break the pot. The reward lies in the pot and the willing shoulders of others is the only way to succeed! This sport answers my question on how a leader can see further, more and before others can, and become 20 feet tall.

Leadership skills are a combination of skills and capabilities that make you a superhuman. A superhuman who is immersed in taking his team towards collective and individual success.

'*The ability to motivate yourself and your team towards achieving a goal, and getting the best out of your team and you, even in adverse circumstances, is leadership.*'

—Dr Vivek Mansingh

As I review vignettes of my leadership moments, the lessons are crystal clear: Leaders produce results, they lead themselves and their teams towards accomplishing goals, and they are able to garner the trust of people. How each leader does it could differ—the facets are clear but the methods may vary. Leaders work hard towards building respect and trust, sharing responsibility, displaying emotional strength, connecting deeply with people, working with discipline and to principles, having a vision, passion and a deeply ingrained ability to persevere through odds. *Sounds like a lot, right?!* It isn't, really.

Not a 'people leader' yet? No problem! ***It is important to understand that leadership is not just for people at the top of an organization, it is for everyone***. I can assure you that if you are displaying these leadership skills, you are moving towards becoming the best version of yourself and will move up the career ladder faster than a person who isn't. That is because you would have earned the leadership position! *True leadership rests in the followers' hearts, not on a business card*. It cannot be awarded, appointed, or assigned. It has to be earned.

> 'When you become a leader, you lose the right to think about yourself.'
>
> —Gerald Brooks

Once, a young leader whom I was mentoring asked me, 'I keep reading books on leadership competencies. But I'd like to know, from your experience, which competencies are important.'

Leaders, I replied, need to have a vision. Vision without action is but a dream, action without vision just passes time, vision with action can change the world.

A leader finds a dream and then people; others find a leader and then the dream.

Vision has to be followed up by a strategy and a huge reserve of positive energy.

Leaders have to be passionate. They should have energy, vitality and enthusiasm in pursuing the vision. Teams cannot be prescribed 'passion' as a dose on a piece of paper or as an instruction in an email. They will become passionate only when they see their leader brimming with passion.

Leaders have to be likeable. People will follow you only if they like you. You can be likeable by placing them first, praising good work and taking the brunt of any harsh feedback received from external sources. You should recognize that nobody is perfect and that each person is different from the other. Everyone likes and needs appreciation. So, give sincere compliments. Whenever you feel like writing or saying something blunt, think about how you would feel on receiving that, and amend your words accordingly.

Leaders develop relationships. They need to touch hearts before they ask for a hand. They should make individual and meaningful ties with all their team members and be genuinely interested in improving people around them. Set aside your ego and be humble and approachable.

Leaders earn respect and trust by keeping their character, value systems and principles impeccable. They exhibit courage and integrity. A powerful way to build trust is to put the team's needs and what's best for them ahead of your personal agenda.

Leaders develop knowledge and skills. If your grip on the subject matter is shallow, you will not be able to earn the team's respect. In this aspect, I am reminded of Padmashree Warrior, who was the CTO at Cisco and my colleague at one point. What set her apart was the depth of her knowledge and, supplementing that, phenomenal presentation skills, down-to-earth openness and passion.

Leaders communicate well. As some experts say, leaders don't convey the message, *they are the message*! Communication does so much beyond informing. It persuades and motivates, shows the path, conveys empathy and also inspires. You must give out more of yourself and allow others a peek into yourself when you are communicating.

Leaders execute. Unless you are achieving results and helping the team do the same, you are on shaky ground.

When you walk into a meeting, people should see you as someone who has decisive and well-worked-out plans and is committed to putting in whatever it takes. Persevere, measure progress and don't rest till you have reached the destination. That builds your brand as a leader.

Success Factors of Leaders

1. Leaders have a powerful vision.
2. Leaders think strategically and have a positive outlook.
3. Leaders are passionate.
4. Leaders are likeable.
5. Leaders develop relationships.
6. Leaders earn respect and trust.
7. Leaders develop knowledge and skills needed to accomplish the mission.
8. Leaders communicate and motivate.
9. Leaders execute well.
10. Leaders create leaders.

I am always asked: are leaders born or made? My answer is that some people may have better inherent leadership skills, *but most leaders are made by sheer determination, hard work and following the thoughts shared in this chapter.* Everyone may not become a world leader, but they will become stronger leaders and the best version of themselves, and accomplish things they never imagined they could. One has to keep in mind that leadership skills are developed over a period of time by relentless focus and effort, not just by reading a book or taking a course. Start small: lead an internship project if you are a student, or lead a small project if you are new in your career. Even a simple initiative like organizing a team-building outing, building or painting a classroom at a local school with your team through your company's giving-back programme can help you build leadership skills. If you are already managing a team, become a stronger leader by developing the leadership skills required to achieve an outcome that looks difficult.

Once again, I am reminded of Mahatma Gandhi and his march to a small town near Surat called Dandi. It was a distance of 385 kilometres. *Why did he walk?* Couldn't he have just complained about the repressive salt tax via a letter? The answer is that *leadership starts where logic stops.* Gandhi charged up millions of souls by walking. Historians call it a 'great catalyst' in the Indian struggle for independence.

When Rama Described Leadership

When the banished Prince Rama prepared to battle the formidable forces of Ravana, the multi-headed demon king of Lanka, Vibhishana, Ravana's younger

contd.

brother, asked him, 'Rama, how are you going to defeat Ravana; you do not have even a chariot!'

Rama replied calmly, 'I have the perfect chariot. It will help us win.' He went on to explain.

- The charioteer is his own self: he is fighting for a noble cause; he has a vision and a clear conscience.
- The four wheels of his chariot are character, courage, ethics and valour.
- The horses are his strength—discernment, hard work, action and perseverance.
- The reins to steer the chariot are forgiveness, compassion, consistency and equanimity.
- The flag on the chariot is marked with honesty and righteousness.
- The armour is his knowledge and credibility.
- The bows and arrows are strategy, intelligence, skills, his firm commitment and restraint on emotions like ego and anger.

Rama smiled gently and said, '*Ehi sam vijay upaya na dooja*' (There is no other way to win).

The leadership journey isn't easy. You will end up annoying some people, especially those who don't like being pushed out of their comfort zone. But, as Steve

Jobs said, 'If you wish to make everyone happy, don't be a leader, sell ice-cream instead!'

I always challenged leaders who worked for me, pushing them towards a level of maturity where they could make sound decisions without my being in the room. I must have ruffled a few feathers in the process. However, I stayed committed to my approach. *My mission was and still remains the same—to create more 'Viveks'.* A good leader will create more leaders through the course of his leadership journey. I endeavour to do the same.

'*I am not afraid of an army of lions led by a sheep; I am afraid of an army of sheep led by a lion.*'
—Alexander the Great

Key Learnings

1. Leadership is not just for people at the top of an organization; it is for everyone.
2. Leadership skills are a combination of skills and capabilities that make you a superhuman being.
3. By developing leadership skills, you will become the best version of yourself, move up the career ladder much faster and achieve bigger things in life.
4. Leadership skills can be developed by consciously and relentlessly following the thoughts shared in this chapter.

Guru Mantra on Leadership: Kiran Mazumdar-Shaw, founder, Biocon

Leadership is about decision-making abilities, critical thinking, leading in crisis, empowering yourself and others. Everyone should build these abilities.

Leadership is not about 'I–me–myself'. It's about how you can get a team to collaborate and solve problems. It's about getting acceptance from your team.

I am a believer in the old adage, 'Lead by example'. Don't say one thing and do another. For example, if I say that integrity and accountability are values dear to me, I have to demonstrate them, too. A leader has to be fair and not show a bias to certain people. I also believe in the leader being accessible to all people; I leave my door wide open. Anyone with an issue can walk in.

Mentee Speaks on Leadership: Sridhar Gaddipati, vice president, Cisco

It was 2010 when Cisco was rapidly expanding its R&D in India, and they brought in Dr Vivek Mansingh as a senior leader. It was not only a defining moment for Cisco India, but also a pivotal moment in my professional career. Vivek and I formed a very close mentor–mentee relationship. He laced mentoring with anecdotes, humour and common sense. For instance, 'Know where you are going; any road is good if you do not know where you are going.'

I learnt leadership by example. I learnt to develop a big vision, strategy, planning, execution, and the distinction between managing and leading teams.

By improving my leadership skills, I first became a director and then a vice president at Cisco, currently managing global teams. I have achieved a much higher level of professional and personal success following the leadership and other lessons I learnt.

ENTREPRENEURSHIP

SEVEN

Entrepreneurship: Changing the World

'A ship in the harbour is safe, but that is not what ships are built for.'

—John A. Shedd

When one thinks of 'industry' in India, the Tata Group, which has more than a hundred operating companies that contribute to more than 4 per cent of India's GDP, is probably the first that comes to mind. And so does the name Jamsetji Tata, who was known as 'the man who saw tomorrow'. With their optimism, persuasiveness, persistence, resourcefulness and determination to control their own destiny even when competing with businesses blessed by the British Raj, I'd say the Tata Group were the first rock star entrepreneurs of India! They transformed themselves from a small trading company, once considered insignificant in Bombay industrial circles, and emerged as the largest indigenously financed and managed industrial group in India.

Since then, India has created the third-largest entrepreneurial ecosystem in the world with more than eighty unicorns (companies of more than $1 billion value) and thousands of healthy, flourishing start-ups and businesses.

Today, India needs an even stronger entrepreneurial ecosystem to find innovative and unique solutions for its problems and, in doing so, create jobs and assist in overall economic development.

As I look back, my own avatar as an entrepreneur was propelled by pure passion. I had this burning need inside to solve a problem that led to the start-ups that I created or was part of. They were ATTI in the US, and Ishoni Networks and Portal Software in India. It has been one of the most rewarding parts of my professional experience. Since then, I have incubated, funded and nurtured numerous start-ups and mentored their founders.

Why Entrepreneurship is so Exciting!

- *Entrepreneurs turn their passion and beliefs into a business.*
- Entrepreneurs can improve the way we live and work, as their products and services can increase our productivity and standard of living.

contd.

- Entrepreneurs have the opportunity to change lives, create jobs and fuel economic development.
- Entrepreneurs have no growth ceiling and have unlimited income potential.
- Entrepreneurs are masters of their (professional) destiny.
- Entrepreneurs learn a staggering amount in just a couple of years, much more than they could learn by taking an MBA.

Entrepreneurship can be a phenomenally exciting career choice for the reasons mentioned in the box. However, entrepreneurship is a different ball game, and not everyone's cup of tea! It is much harder than a safe nine-to-five job, I'd say. It is highly demanding; hence, in addition to the required skills and hard work, one must possess mental and emotional toughness.

To put it simply, if you are an entrepreneur, the buck stops with you. That adds many action items to your bubbling pot of deliverables and several stressors, as well. What makes it even more challenging is:

- The fact that this is a marathon you are running, not a sprint.
- There's always a fire to fight, often multiple ones that simultaneously pull you in different directions.

- You're working 24/7 and eight days a week! To make it worse, uncertainty looms large and even your company's survival can be at stake during tough times.
- In all likelihood, you're competing with the best, often bigger players who have more resources than you do.

To add to it, there is no trusted recipe for success you could follow. Every situation is unique, so you can't just copy a method that worked for someone else.

I strove to learn from the best but was careful not to make the mistake of 'cutting and pasting' their views into my context. I applied their tips to my entrepreneurship puzzle with a conscious astuteness.

Steve Jobs said: 'Customers are not supposed to know what they need.' Somewhat contradictorily, Jeff Bezos says, 'Work backwards from customer needs to know what to build next.' *Does that confuse you?* It shouldn't! One needs to understand that both ideas work remarkably well if you consider them in light of the type and stages their businesses were in when those statements were made. Michael Dell says, 'Ideas are a commodity. Execution of them is not.' However, John Chambers of Cisco says, 'Market transitions create unique ideas around which big business can be built.' Again, these two views might seem diametrically opposed but aren't if viewed in the context in which they were spoken. So, in summary, do learn from the world's most successful entrepreneurs and others but never cut and paste their suggestions to your business; pick what is relevant to you at each point in time.

While entrepreneurship has its challenges, it is also a great opportunity, if you have the right qualities mentioned in the box.

Qualities Successful Entrepreneurs Have

In the course of working with hundreds of entrepreneurs and reflecting on my own experience, all the qualities that have been mentioned in the book—passion, excellence, creativity and innovation, leadership, subject-matter knowledge, mentorship—are important for entrepreneurs.

However, in addition, this breed of dynamic folk needs these additional qualities.

1. Risk-taking ability
2. Ability to deal with uncertainty
3. Persuasiveness
4. Persistence
5. Resourcefulness
6. Optimism
7. A strong sense of responsibility for decisions

---

contd.

8. High levels of energy, great perseverance and a sense of imagination
9. Highly contagious enthusiasm
10. An ability to convey a sense of purpose and inspire action

So, what does it take to be successful as an entrepreneur? While entrepreneurship really requires a widespread buffet of skills and attitudes, akin to feeding an *always hungry* baby, there are ten that I have picked as the most essential ones. I call them the Ten Commandments for Entrepreneurs.

The Ten Commandments for Entrepreneurs

Commandment 1: Thou shalt have passion

You need to be extremely passionate about your idea and the venture that ensues. It will tear you away from most areas of your life, and you'll spend some of your most productive years in a pressure-cooker environment. You will spend less or even no time on things other than work. *Imagine having to tell the spouse and the kids that the planned vacation needs to be cancelled!* At work, there will be moments of exultation and moments of crisis. The only thing that will keep you going is passion. So, you'd better have tremendous commitment and be obsessed with the problem you are solving.

Commandment 2: Thou shalt know thy space in and out

Understand your product or solution space extremely well. Study the competition thoroughly. Do not take your competition lightly. They are as smart as you are and may have more resources. Learn from them. Set aside a substantial amount of time and effort to understand the competitive landscape and to study role-model companies (in or outside your industry) in order to offer a differentiated, strong and sustainable value proposition. The biggest trap you need to watch out for is confirmation bias—the tendency to search for, interpret, favour and recall information that confirms or supports what you want to believe.

Commandment 3: Thou shalt hunger for market feedback

While a strong conviction in yourself and your product is a good thing, being open to feedback from customers, the market and the competition is indispensable. I recall spending time with an entrepreneur who would ask for feedback but the moment my feedback deviated from his preferred zone of praise, he'd become defensive, shuffle his feet and lose interest in the conversation. He needed to be more open to new ideas, primarily because I have rarely seen a start-up exit with the same business plan, product or solution with which they started the venture.

Commandment 4: Thou shalt be an engaging storyteller

Your narration should be so engaging that it should paint a picture and galvanize people into action. Practise in front of the mirror: build an impressive sixty-second elevator pitch. When you open your mouth to speak, it should be like someone has lifted the lid of a box of the city's best pizza in front of a group of starving people. This skill will help you not only in raising money but also in recruiting top talent, motivating your team, building partnerships and, of course, selling.

Commandment 5: Thou shalt get some good mentors

You could get yourself one trusted mentor or, perhaps, multiple ones for different aspects of your work. At least one mentor should have 'been there, done that'. Make sure you listen to them without your ego or defences getting in the way. Allow the mentor to be brutal, to say things that you may not want to hear.

Commandment 6: Thou shalt build a strong organization

While almost all entrepreneurs agree that a solid organization with solid people is important, very few actually prioritize it at the beginning. Talent determines the potential of your venture. Your policies for engagement and growth will determine the morale; a carefully planned structure will be the bedrock for planning scalability, and your stated values and vision will be the compass to lead people. While you can be informal and flexible at the start, do not make the mistake of ignoring the importance of structure and processes for your organization.

Commandment 7: Thou shalt create a winning culture

John Chambers says that a CEO's biggest job is to create a winning culture. As a leader, if you haven't thought about the kind of culture you wish to create, and aren't articulating it as frequently as you communicate targets, you are missing the opportunity to create something long-lasting and high-performing. Razor-sharp clarity on your desired culture is absolutely essential. It could be as simple as 'Customer First', 'Quality First', 'Bad News First'; whichever inspires your team to do what you care about automatically, on their own and without compromise.

Commandment 8: Thou shalt keep the creativity quotient high and foster innovation

It is innovation that will give your start-up a sustainable competitive advantage. Without doubt, a constant nudge towards thinking originally, and unencumbered by the boundaries of the business is important. Let your team challenge the status quo and think out of the box. If you find yourself not saying 'no way' a bit too often to mundane and predictable solutions, you are building a culture that inhibits innovation. You should build 'innovative idea generation' as part of your planning, execution and review meetings. *And never forget to reward innovation!* Create intellectual property and file patents that address the core of your product as soon as possible in the life of your ventures.

Commandment 9: Thou shalt be an effective manager to manage flawless execution

As the great management consultant Peter Drucker prescribes, there is NO alternative to this foolproof method of managing: setting goals (for your team and yourself), developing detailed plans, executing with rigour, measuring progress (milestones and productivity), achieving goals/milestones and celebrating and appreciating.

Commandment 10: Thou shalt persevere

Starting up and nurturing the business is like a walk in the park. Just that the park has a fire raging at one end and a tornado approaching from the other! Yes, starting up a business is tough! A lot of start-ups come face to face with annihilation. *My message is: persevere—do not open the parachute and admit defeat unless you have given it everything you have!*

The commandments are simple and tested. With these under your belt and your sight on the stars, no one can stop you. Think big from the start and even bigger as you scale up. As Kiran Mazumdar-Shaw says, 'I want to be remembered as someone who put India on the scientific map of the world in terms of large innovation. I want to be remembered for making a difference to global healthcare. And I want to be remembered as someone who did make a difference to social economic development in India.'

Shradha Sharma of YourStory, which has been the cradle for over 40,000 entrepreneurs' narratives since its inception and a start-up that is much talked about, often shares about how the entrepreneurial journey is bittersweet. It's not for those who are shaken up easily! I would agree with that.

Pushed Outside the Comfort Zone

I still remember the day when I met Dr Mansingh to discuss the landscaping for his new house. I was a struggling landscaper with a team of about four. He saw my passion and deep knowledge and gave me the contract. When we started working with him, I learnt how particular he was about the finer details, symmetry and balance. It was a small, personal garden but it became the biggest canvas for me to learn from.

We never formed a formal mentoring relationship but I became a mentee and he, my guru. Initially, I would approach him with a list of what I considered 'problems of my growing business'. He'd wave them off, saying they weren't real problems. He'd say, 'Look for bigger problems.' I would try to impress him by getting a bigger problem, but it never worked. I learnt a deep lesson: that if one has to achieve something big, the problems one has to take head-on should also be big.

He told me that the great depth of subject matter I had was awesome. It gave me a lot of self-confidence. He helped me 'think big'. I rediscovered my creativity and developed excellence. Today, I have a team of 500 and a name that is known across India.

—Pradeep, Garden World

So, ready to build your start-up? If you are a college student and would like to create your own start-up, your wheel of goals may look like an example shared in the appendix. For others, is there a structured way of building a start-up? Yes, here are seven simple steps you can take to get your dream venture off the ground.

Building Your Start-up in Seven Steps

Step 1: Find an idea

The imperative that births ideas are unsolved problems that have made you excited about creating unique solutions that are significantly (*not marginally*) better than existing products/solutions. iPhone, Tesla, Byju's, Freshworks, BigBasket are all good examples. Are you passionate about the space and area of your start-up? You will be working for five to ten years in this area, so you'd better be! Make sure your product has a ***strong differentiated value proposition that can be sustained over a long period of time*** (40 per cent of start-ups fail because of a poor value proposition).

Step 2: Do a thorough competitive analysis

An understanding of the competitive landscape is extremely important. Many founders gloss over this and face adverse consequences. You need to ask yourself how your competitors' solutions address the problem your product seeks to resolve. When you arrive at a list of those, don't dismiss them but seek to understand them as much as you would dissect and understand your own product. Many young entrepreneurs tell me that their idea is unique and there is no direct competition. Let me tell you that I have not come across any start-up that does not have healthy competition. If you happen to be in a situation where competition is limited, it is important to analyse the entry barriers in the product market space that you are working in, to be able to assess the possibility of future competition. *Only when you know the competition well can you come up with a differentiated value proposition which will be the key to your success.* Competitive analysis is not a one-time exercise; you have to devote a decent amount of time to continuously track your competition. Also, **identify a role model company and learn from their journey**. Remember, 'Success leaves clues,' says Anthony Robbins.

Step 3: Know your Total Available Market (TAM)

This step means that you do a clean and honest estimation of your market. *Deep and clever segmentation is a MUST for a start-up.* You will be spread too thin if you endeavour to challenge your competition in broad markets. So, you need to be incisively sharp in the segment you are offering the unique value proposition. The Internet of

Things (IoT) may be a trillion-dollar market, but you need to consider the specific segment you would be addressing. In that segment, what is *your* TAM? If you have overestimated or wrongly understood your available market, you are making yourself susceptible to problems related to product configuration, product positioning and, in fact, the business model itself. So, know your TAM and segment very clearly before you sharpen your product or solution.

Step 4: Create a solid business plan and raise seed money

Investors look for strong founders with integrity, passion, commitment, optimism, industry and segment knowledge, a clear vision, and a huge cache of potential. They will be listening keenly to figure out how strong and differentiated your value proposition is and how you intend to build your business. While friends, family and angel investors would be the best sources of funds at this stage, make sure you have a powerful business plan in place that captures all aspects of your business over the next three to five years.

Step 5: Create a stellar product or solution and get early customers

Simplicity and user experience are extremely important. Make sure that you create intellectual property, as it installs a barrier to entry for others. It is also important to test the market by introducing a Minimum Viable Product (MVP) as soon as possible by getting a few pilot customers first or, even better, paying customers. This initial validation also helps minimize the entrepreneur's initial biases and reach the right product–market fit early on.

Step 6: Create a business model

Create a business model indicating exactly how you will be delivering value to the customers. Make sure your business model is cash-flow efficient, has as many variable costs as possible, is capital-light wherever possible and is scalable. Look for opportunities for innovation in your business model. A good and unique business model will not only give your business a boost but can also provide an entry barrier for others.

Step 7: Scale your business

As the business scales, focus on these three pillars:

Pillar 1: Building strong internal teams with three gods

The most important hires will be in your product or solution space. *Focus on the three gods of the technology team—product manager, industrial designer/*

user experience leader and technical architect. Make sure these are A-class people, the best talent you can find. Because these three people will define the potential success of your venture, especially if your venture is in the technology area.

In addition, make sure you get the right folk for customer service, marketing, sales and support, and finance, compliance and legal. Don't just look at their résumés—make sure you get the people with the same values and fire in the belly as yours!

Pillar 2: Building external partnerships

Building channels to take your products and services to customers is a critical success factor. I have witnessed many entrepreneurs expending precious energy managing poorly selected suppliers, distributors and resellers. Ask around and make sure you consider a positive word-of-mouth before making your choices.

Pillar 3: Growing the business

Seek to penetrate deeper into the market with your existing products. When the time is right, expand into new products and geographies. In this, it is important to anticipate changes in the business models associated with new products or geographies.

Soon, it will be time to raise successive rounds of funds from venture capitalists and if you have ticked the boxes in each of the seven steps as shown, you will have investors lining up.

What VCs Look at

1. You (who they invest in)
2. Openness to being coached
3. Integrity, passion, commitment
4. Experience, domain expertise
5. Skills (tech, marketing, sales, finance)
6. Team with a diverse skill set
7. A clear vision and great potential
8. A strongly differentiated value proposition
9. Validation
10. No BS (they see through it!)

I have mentioned it earlier also and would like to repeat this common hurdle: most start-ups do face a near-death experience sometime in their life. You will feel like you are flying a rickety airplane in bumpy weather, maybe parts of it are falling apart, and you are gasping for air at that altitude.

My advice: keep flying, don't open the parachute as a response to panic until you have given it all you have.

You will never lose; you will either succeed or you will learn!

'The difference between a stumbling block and a stepping stone is how high you raise your foot.'

—Benny Lewis

Key Learnings

1. Entrepreneurship may not be for everyone; but if you have what it takes, it is a fantastic career path that offers a tremendous opportunity to leave your mark.
2. The first critical step is to find an idea and create a business plan that captures all aspects of your business, particularly its long-term viability.
3. Once that exercise has given you a strong conviction, go and play a solid innings with the ideas shared in this chapter, giving it everything you've got.

Guru Mantra on Entrepreneurship from Ratan Tata, chairman, Tata Group

More than ability, I have valued attitude, maturity and seriousness of founders. That meant more to me than any other single factor. Fire in the belly is needed, inventing a better way to do something is important, as is being particular about not going ahead if there are ethical issues, and finally, the courage and tenacity to see it through.

Guru Mantra on Entrepreneurship from Vani Kola, founder, Kalaari Capital

The five skills entrepreneurs need are conviction, ability to listen, grit, being purpose-driven and open to continuous learning.

Mentee Speaks on Entrepreneurship: Sneh Vaswani, founder and CEO, Miko

We at Miko fondly have a term for Dr Mansingh's words of advice: 'gems of wisdom'. They have been remarkably useful in helping us build Miko and catalysing my own successes. I remember my first meeting with Dr Mansingh in 2017. I had come prepared with a typical VC pitch deck for our Pre-Series A. He gently brushed it aside and, instead, took a two-hour deep dive into the product and technology. I was very impressed with the sheer quality of our interaction, his understanding of global consumer products and ability to go from the 30,000-feet view to the minute nitty-gritty of user experience and technology. I developed a new respect for the importance of deep expertise and excellence.

Soon, no trip to Bangalore was complete without meeting Dr Mansingh to seek inputs on a variety of areas spanning go-to-market, product, marketing and sales. The insights on entrepreneurship, including competitive analysis, TAM and driving unique value proposition have helped in making Miko successful in 140+ countries. I also learnt the significance of excellence in my products driven by innovation.

INSPIRER ROLE MODEL MENTOR BOOKS

YOU NEED FOUR MORE GODS

EIGHT

You Need Four More Gods

'A good mentor will help you see where you can reach instead of focusing on where you are.'

—Dr Vivek Mansingh

I like walking on the dew-drenched grass on my lawn each morning, soaking in the chirping of birds, the scent of roses and the freshness of the morning breeze. As I do so, I reflect on god and his blessings. Time spent dwelling inside oneself can be a great mind-opener.

While the Almighty has always been a powerful figure in my life, **I have learnt that one needs four more gods right here on this planet**. These are forces who will shape you into becoming the best version of yourself. *Even if you haven't met them!* That's a supernatural quality, hence the word 'gods'. And, just as one approaches the supreme being, one needs to approach these gods, too, with humility, openness, submission and discipline. The benediction that you will receive will be magical, almost miraculous. But only if you seek them with all your heart and soul. *These four gods are inspirers, role models, mentors and books.*

Inspirers

Firstly, there are the **inspirers**. *These are embodiments of talent, achievement and strong character in any field—* not necessarily in your own. So, while you may not be striving to be a music composer like A.R. Rahman or an IT leader like Michael Dell, there are remarkable facets about them that you can pick up as nuggets. I, for instance, was greatly inspired by Dr A.P.J. Abdul Kalam and admired his leadership qualities, his passion for excellence, grand vision for India and, above all, his humility. I salute Jeff Bezos for an entire industry that he has created. Rahul Dravid has been a god, I am sure, not only for me but a lot of you as well. Now, while I was never on the path to becoming a cricketer, I have always marvelled at his pursuit of perfection and unblemished integrity. I have internalized the hallmarks of these great people. Every single day, I try, with a fluid and clear consciousness, to learn from the greats. I glean from their talks and books the ideas that inspire me. I make well-weighed-up plans to implement what I learn.

Role Models

Secondly, there are the **role models**. *Very simply put, you want to be just like them!* When you are young, you look up to seniors in the family. It could be a parent, teacher, cousin, uncle or aunt who has achieved something marvellous.

Take a minute to think—who is your role model? *Having a role model is as important as having a blueprint before you start constructing a building.* A person you regard highly can influence your thoughts and actions to great lengths, if you internalize him or her as a role model.

You will be filled with a spark, giving you the impetus to reach the next level. Think of it: all great leaders, sportsmen and high achievers have role models whom they strive to emulate.

A given role model may not stay forever. As we grow and transition to different phases of our lives, different people become more relevant as role models. In fact, you could have more than one role model at any given point in time.

I have come across so many stories on the power of emulation, one being of Ben Kingsley, a British actor, who was chosen to play a mega-icon of India: Gandhi. There were so many ways in which he could have got it all wrong. But he was determined to prove to himself and to the world that he was the best choice to provide an authentic portrayal of the great man. As the film crew prepared to begin shooting, Ben Kingsley decided to take this 'awesomely scary and intimidating' mission head-on. He read twenty-eight books on the Mahatma. He changed his meals to mimic what Gandhi ate. His mornings began early with yoga and meditation, while the evenings were spent in learning to spin the charkha or spinning wheel. He not only learnt how to spin the wheel but also experienced how that act made one stronger and more patient. This role modelling helped him 'feel' like the man he was portraying, and he started thinking and behaving like Gandhi. No wonder, he and the movie won a bucketful of Oscar awards. That's the power of a role model!

How do you select your role models? By reading about them, listening to their talks and reading their books. They are generally in your professional area of interest.

Mentors

The third god you need is a **mentor**. *Mentors are successful, knowledgeable, compassionate people who have, ideally, 'been there, done that'*. While role models can be people who may or may not be accessible to you, mentors are those who can be there with you more often.

Think of them as the navigators on the vehicle you are driving. If you listen to them, they will get you where you need to be!

While you don't need to have any relationship with an inspirer or a role model, you need a relationship with a mentor. This relationship needs to be built on *mutual respect, trust, shared values and honest communication*. However qualified and wise a prospective mentor is, you cannot have him or her as a mentor if, for any reason, your relationship lacks any of these.

Mentors have a depth of experience available for you to tap, like a tree ripe and dripping with resin. They can facilitate your professional and personal development, and also offer encouragement, counselling and support in addition to wisdom. They have to be generous with their time, connections and other resources they can bestow upon you.

As you search for mentors, think about your former managers and colleagues, alumni, professors, family, friends and online mentoring offerings.

Think about the key qualities, values and personality characteristics you are looking for in a mentor before you start your search. Mentors and coaches should have business expertise and be able to understand the environment and challenges of the mentee. *You wouldn't use a tennis coach for cricket, would you?*

However, there is a possibility that an amazing mentor ends up proving to be entirely useless! That happens when the mentee hasn't humbled themselves enough to learn. As a mentee, one has to have the hunger to learn, to persevere and get it right. You have to be curious, organized, efficient, responsible and engaged. Sometimes a mentor may tell you things that you don't like, things that shake you up or upset you. Do you have it in you to take all of their words in the right spirit?

Successful mentoring starts with a *powerful end mission statement* clarifying what you are looking for from this mentoring experience.

From your mentor, seek guidance about life in general, advice about career, roadblocks and obstacles you are facing. Ask for professional guidance. Don't hesitate in running past them ethical or moral conundrums that are bothering you. To extract the most out of your meetings, do plan an agenda ahead of meetings and make sure that your mentor has adequate time in advance to review any related materials.

My Mentors

My first mentor was my uncle, Dr Abhai Mansingh.

My second mentor was my PhD supervisor, Prof. P. Oosthuizen.

Then my mentor was my manager at HP, David Horine.

After that my mentor was Dr Avram Bar-Cohen.

Post that, my mentor was Bart Patel, founder and CEO of Fluent.

Then my mentor was Prakash Bhalerao, a billionaire serial entrepreneur.

Later, a mentor and inspirer, among others, was John Chambers of Cisco.

My current mentors are two successful VCs, and Ramesh and Swati Ramanathan for my non-profit efforts.

---

contd.

As my career evolved, my mentors also changed. Many of the people who were my inspiration became my role models and then my mentors as I moved up the ladder in my career. Dr Avram Ben-Cohen and Prakash Bhalerao are two such examples.

I have also been reverse-mentored by Satish MM, an outstanding technical professional who has worked with me for many years, and my sons, Anant and Ayush. Take reverse mentoring seriously; you can learn a lot.

Often, the terms 'mentor' and 'coach' are used interchangeably. There is a major difference, though. Coaching is directed towards improving a specific aspect of performance and is generally oriented towards the short term, while mentoring is a longer-term, more holistic development-driven engagement which may include professional as well as other areas of life.

If you find yourself slipping in some areas of performance, do reach out to someone to coach you. Every top athlete in the world has a coach, whether it is Roger Federer, Mary Kom or P.V. Sindhu. Imagine if these people, who are already reigning in their fields, are benefited by having a coach or mentor, how much more ordinary people like us can.

A book that I really like is *Trillion Dollar Coach*. Bill Campbell was a football coach who, after working in tech, turned executive coach for the who's who of Silicon

Valley's elite leaders, such as Steve Jobs, Eric Schmidt, Larry Page and Sergey Brin, to name some. This humble man, who remains largely unknown, changed the lives of some of the world's biggest leaders. The stories and eye-opening lessons can really impact you. Do read the book and learn from it till you figure out your own coach and mentor. ***If some of the world's best leaders can benefit from mentors, why not mere mortals like us?***

What is in it for mentors? An ancient Buddhist proverb says, *'If you light a lamp for someone, it will also brighten your own path.'* Having mentored a lot of people, I can tell you that in every interaction, I have also learnt something.

Imprints on the Heart

It must have been almost five years after settling down in India when I got a call from James*, a former colleague (who directly reported to me) from California. He said he was coming to India for two days and wanted to meet me. I was delighted. 'Of course, come over when you're done with your work in India!' He replied, 'I don't have any work. I am coming just to meet you!' I was stumped.

As a leader, one nugget of gold that I have picked up is that you can't move people to action unless

---

*name changed   *contd.*

you first move them with emotion: the heart comes before the head. You might be knowledgeable and brilliant, but people don't care how much you know until they know how much you care.

To earn their respect, put them ahead of yourself, place their needs and aspirations before yours, make sound decisions in things that affect the team and, most importantly, admit your mistakes when you make one!

When James arrived, we had two days of mentoring sessions on life's goal-setting, potential career paths, developing leadership skills and excellence in his area of expertise, which both of us enjoyed thoroughly. I was blown over when he told me, 'I have your photo in my home. Whenever I am faced with a complicated situation, I just look at it and ask, "How would Vivek go about it?"' So, a mentor can guide and inspire, even when he is not physically present!

Books

This brings me to the fourth god: **books** (including audio books, podcasts and videos).

'The man who does not read good books has no advantage over the man who can't read them.'

—Mark Twain

This is as true as the reflection you see in the mirror each day. Reading helps you grow mentally, emotionally and psychologically, it keeps you updated and makes you smarter. It improves your writing ability by gifting you a larger vocabulary. But the sad truth is that the reading habit is declining. In fact, people will spend Rs 250 on a mug of frappuccino but will groan if asked to do the same on a book. While coffee can stimulate you for a brief period, reading gives your brain a brisk workout. This happens because parts of the brain such as vision, language and associative learning connect in a specific neural circuit for the purpose of reading. A study by the University of Sussex found that reading for just six minutes can reduce stress levels by up to 68 per cent. Other studies have reported that reading provides the same benefits as meditation. To get the most out of a book, you can write a review or present the summary of the book to your family, friends or colleagues. I used to discuss business books in my staff meetings and encouraged my staff to read and present the summary.

Most successful people are proficient book-readers and acknowledge the role reading books has played in their success. *I highly recommend that you read at least one book a month in your professional area of interest.* Let me share my journey with books: I learnt pretty early in my career that one needs to reskill frequently given the rapid changes in technology. Books became my teachers to help me enhance my subject-matter expertise. As I built on this habit, I read about people who inspired me and learnt from their lives. It may be hard to reach Dr A.P.J Abdul Kalam or Narayana Murthy, but reading their biographies and books can throw open a beautiful window into their lives and the lessons residing in them. I had promised my younger self to read twenty to thirty books each year. The nature of the books kept changing as my trajectory changed. So, while the initial ones were in the area of technology, soon, I was reading books on innovation. I particularly enjoyed *The Innovator's Dilemma*. I went on to read on leadership and have enjoyed books by Jack Welch and Stephen Covey. *Who Says Elephants Can't Dance* was a bottle-opener that unlocked so many areas of awareness in my mind. So was *Built to Last* and *Blink*. When I began to work with start-ups, I read many relevant books, my favourites being *Start-up Nation*, *Zero to One* and *Hard Things about Hard Things*. I read books on finance (John C. Bogle, Peter Lynch and Warren Buffet) to keep my financial acumen sharpened. Books by or about my favourite leaders—John Chambers, Satya Nadella, Narayana Murthy, Nandan Nilekani, Michael Dell, Steve Jobs, Andrew Grove, to name a few—have a place on my bookshelf and in my heart.

In this phase of life, I am reading pretty voraciously about the world of venture capitalists. *Mastering the VC Game* has been immensely useful. I love reading books that touch the soul. *Autobiography of a Yogi* is one such book and so is literature on inner engineering by Sadhguru.

All Four Gods in One

It was a sunny afternoon in San Diego and I had reached the bronze and shale-coloured hotel well before time. My heart was fluttering as if a hundred butterflies had infiltrated all four chambers within it! I was nervous—in an excited sort of way! I was going to meet a 'god' that day. Not really meet, though—just hear him speak. Dr Avram Ben-Cohen, one of the highest regarded professionals in the field of electronics cooling, was speaking. I had read his book which was considered the Bible in that area.

He was giving a keynote address at a conference I was attending. I entered the conference room well in advance, armed with my notepad and pen, like an eager kid. In just a few minutes, GOD entered! A modestly built man, dressed in a simple shirt and trousers. I sprang to my feet to applaud him. His presentation began. I was rapt, like an attentive schoolboy. After the talk, I jostled through the crowd, trying to reach him to get a chance to speak with him. I think I was only able to say that I admired him and enjoyed his talk.

contd.

Over the years, I remained a huge fan of his depth of knowledge and excellence in his field. Not to mention his humility and approachability. I tried to learn and copy all his traits.

He became my inspirer, then my role model, then my mentor, and later on, at many conferences, we presented technical papers at the same sessions. He complimented me many times on my work at Apple (iMac), my articles and my patents. For me, he was all four gods in one!

Gods aren't meant to be locked away in temples, mosques and churches. We need to keep them in our hearts and lives. The same holds true for these four gods. *They will help you become the best version of yourself.*

Key Learnings

1. Inspirers are people who have certain traits that you admire even though you do not necessarily want to follow their chosen path. The key is to learn and practise the qualities you admire about these inspirers.
2. Having good role models in your life is very important; they influence your actions and thoughts and motivate you to become like them.
3. A mentor is usually an experienced individual who shares knowledge, experience and advice with a less

experienced person or mentee. Everyone must have one or more mentors.

4. Start reading at least twelve books a year that relate to your professional and other areas of interest. You will propel yourself and your career to the next orbit of success.

5. These four gods will help you become the best version of yourself.

Guru Mantra on Mentoring: John Chambers, chairman and CEO, Cisco

We all need mentors. Instead of making your own mistakes, learn from others', that's less painful! I have had mentors all my life, from my parents to my teachers, industry leaders and world leaders. Needless to say, my life has been positively impacted by each one of them.

Guru Mantra on Mentoring: Dr Devi Shetty, cardiac surgeon and chairman, Narayana Health

Let me share a thought on role models. Immediately after Tenzing Norgay and Edmund Hillary scaled Mount Everest, there was a flood of people replicating their feat in a very short time! Mount Everest hadn't changed. People hadn't suddenly become stronger. Those things had remained the same. It is just that someone had proven that it was doable and had become a role model.

That became a huge inspiration. That's the power of role models.

Mentee Speaks on Four Gods: Saurav Agarwala, co-founder and CTO, CRON AI

'Inspirers, role models, mentors and books can be goldmines that can enrich you and one can benefit from each in their journey to success,' says Dr Vivek Mansingh. He calls them the four gods and they have been nothing less than godly for me. My life has and is transforming and getting enriched every day by acting on this advice.

Every entrepreneur wants to make it big and yet, very few get to live this dream. I have found role models not only for myself but also for my company. Since then, my start-up's and my success trajectory have improved dramatically.

TAKE OWNERSHIP OF
YOUR WELL-BEING

GRAND PARENTS

FRIENDS & SIBLINGS

CHILDREN

FATHER

MOTHER

RELATIONSHIPS MATTER MOST

Relationships: What Matter Most

'Relationships are the most valuable assets we have.'
—Dr Vivek Mansingh

'Mom, can you help me make this Lego plane?' Shalini's second-grader came running to her.

'Sorry, not now.' Shalini put her finger on her lips and waved to the nanny to take the child as she logged in to a call.

'You are always working.' The little one made a face.

Shalini would feel sad but there was so much going on at work with the new merger. She just didn't have any time on her hands!

Her children, aged ten and seven, would protest almost every day and then sulk. At thirty-seven, Shalini was doing exceptionally well in her career; she was a technical whiz-kid, a product manager in a well-known company. Her husband, Kumar, was a senior marketing executive in a similar organization. Their lives were busy, every waking hour filled with calls and meetings. In fact, she always joked that she wore her earbuds more than she wore any jewellery! Time for children and family became a lower priority. There is always tomorrow to make it up, she thought. They were planning their annual vacation, this time to Greece, when Shalini was diagnosed with colon cancer.

It was as if an armoured truck had hit them. As if the roof of their house had somehow collapsed on them. Everything came to a standstill. A long course of treatment began—surgery, chemotherapy and radiation. Finally, Shalini was cancer-free and fit to resume life. But, in these months, she had thought deep and hard, 'What is life?' She had found an answer buried deep inside—it's about the people you care for, your family and your friends.

Today, Shalini has all the time her children need. She has taken a role that allows more flexibility. She loves to drive her children to family picnics that are sometimes planned and at other times, quite impromptu.

'Hey, I can also do that trick on the swing,' one can hear her laughing in the park.

Take a moment and pose this question to yourself: *'What would I start doing differently if I had only one year left to live? Only one month?'*

This exercise will give you clarity, in a flash, on the importance of relationships in your life and the people you need to build relationships with. Humans are social animals. At birth, the tender first relationship between the baby and the mother has a tremendous influence on the child. Researchers have observed that brain activity across the 'social brain'—that is, the sum of neuronal networks that makes us relationship-focused—is stronger for kids who received more tactile attention from their mothers. We have an innate need to be close to other people, and relationships with family and friends are one of the greatest sources of happiness in life. The relationships we form with other people are vital to our well-being, our mental and physical health. ***Healthy relationships provide a solid platform from which you can pursue your other life goals***.

As professional recognition and material goals take precedence, people tend to ignore relationship goals. 'I will come back to those later,' is the common mindset. But as the years fly by, those relationships wilt like flowers that haven't been watered. Sometimes, it's too late to revive them. Also, the joy that comes in relishing the relationships cannot be relived. Many successful people have not done so well on the relationship front and were later ready to exchange their professional success for better relationships with loved ones. Prof. Clayton's Harvard students' example, shared in the first chapter, highlights this challenge as well.

Besides, point-in-time is critical for many relationships; your child might need you to be there and mentored more actively in her teens and young adulthood. You can't put that away 'for later'.

As Barack Obama said, 'I am positive that if I'm lucky enough to live to a ripe old age and I'm on my deathbed and I'm thinking back on my life, I won't be remembering some speech I gave or some law I signed—I'll be remembering holding hands with one of my daughters and walking them to a park. That'll be the thing most precious to me.'

Sometimes, it is not that people don't care about relationship goals. It's just that the results of those goals are not as clear and visible as, say, a career goal. So, perhaps unknowingly and inadvertently, they allocate most of their best resources to goals that give tangible results, like professional or material goals.

Your family is the centrepiece of your life. *You can be replaced at work in the blink of an eye, your friends can easily move on, but you are at the centre of your family and cannot be replaced*. Hence, you have to give your best as a husband, wife, son, daughter, sibling, father or mother. Relationships not managed well are the biggest source of regret in life and can cause a lot of stress, pain and unhappiness.

An important piece of advice to young people who are not married yet is to select your partner very carefully. The right partner can propel you to the next orbit; however, an incompatible partner can drag you back, just like in the game of Snakes and Ladders! There is a snake at number 99; if you get there, you land at 10 and need to start all over again.

I am happy I don't have any regrets at this stage of my life. A proud moment for me was when a co-alumnus from Queen's University, Gururaj 'Desh' Deshpande, a serial entrepreneur and self-made billionaire in the US, asked the audience at a session at a TiE—The Indus Entrepreneur—Global Conference that we were both addressing, 'Is there any way to measure what Vivek did for his parents by giving up his career that was at its peak in the USA to return to India to take care of them?' The answer is that there isn't any way of measuring the value of your relationships!

Professional relationships are important too. Networking and thereby creating relationships in your professional field is critical to your long-term professional success. It requires some serious investment of time to keep in touch with alumni and ex-colleagues and make new contacts. People ask me how I built my extensive network. Well, just be genuinely interested in knowing about others, learning from them and helping them as needed. *I always say, don't hesitate in taking help from people in your network, but never forget it and pay it back by helping other people who come to you for help.* You may not have the opportunity to return the favour to the same person who helped you, but carry it forward by helping others. If you ask for favours without gratitude, people see through your overtures pretty quickly!

For building a healthy network in your professional area of interest, present your work at webinars and conferences to contribute and be known in your field (create a brand for yourself). But, like anything that is of value, these relationships need to be fostered with a generous infusion of time and effort.

Ever heard the phrase 'lonely in a crowd'? That happens when you have multiple superficial friendships but no deep ones! Having good friends can enrich one's life and give a lot of happiness. Research suggests that if you have strong friendships, you'll probably find it easier to handle whatever life throws at you. Friends will support you through challenges, give you constructive criticism, make you laugh, and help you become a better version of yourself. Not to mention the benefits to mental as well as physical health. Surround yourself with successful, positive people whom you want to become like. ***Generally, you as a professional and human being are the average of five people you spend a lot of time with***. Preeti and I made a rule a long time back that we would make friends with people whom we admire and from whom we could learn a few things. Avoid socializing and spending time with negative people at all costs.

The philosopher Aristotle said, 'In poverty and other misfortunes of life, true friends are a sure refuge. They keep the young out of mischief, they comfort and aid the old in their weakness, and they incite those in the prime of life to noble deeds.' Studies have shown that older people with close friends are less likely to develop chronic diseases such as heart disease, diabetes and depression than their lonely counterparts.

The nature of the changing times poses several challenges to building and sustaining relationships. These days, people are so entangled in their own affairs that they hardly have any interaction with other family members and friends. Increased use of social media is connecting people like never before but is resulting in less face-to-face interaction and a surfeit of shallow relationships. This is not a very healthy trend and is the cause of rising occurrences of anxiety, depression and other related disorders.

In my life's journey, there were times when I was completely caught up in my professional pursuits. When I ventured into the start-up world, I can recall many days when my family had dinner without me and many months when I could not devote adequate time to them. I am sure it has happened to you, too, sometime or the other. There will be periods when one goal overshadows the rest. It's not a problem as long as you are cognizant of it and come back to the other goals at the earliest.

With this philosophy, I was able to build strong relationships with my parents, wife, sons, immediate and extended family and friends. I had a goal to make my parents and children proud of me. Looking back, I can proudly say that one of the best decisions I made was to return from the US to take care of my ailing mother. Later, I set aside time to be with my father in his sunset years, even though I missed out on career opportunities back in the US. I could make this difficult transition only because I had clarity on my relationship goals.

'Be what you want your children to be.'
—Dr Vivek Mansingh

No one cares for children more than parents. However, when you mentor them, play only one role at a time: you are either a parent or a mentor at a given time. Have you watched the movie *Dangal*? The character Mahavir, the aged wrestler who missed his chance at winning a medal in his heyday, is coaching his daughter Babita to fulfil that dream. As a coach, he is brutal, even merciless, I'd say. But when the coaching hours are over, he goes back to being a loving father; massaging her aching muscles and caring for her nutrition and rest. He knew which hat to wear at what point.

I remember sitting down with a thirteen-year-old Anant, who was in Grade 8, to do a 'college goal-setting' exercise. He said, 'I don't even know where I am headed, Dad.' He was sceptical about the benefits of the exercise. But I persisted. I asked him to write down the names of five colleges that he aspired to join and the five things he needed to do in order to get admission there. Once we had them fleshed out, I guided him towards achieving that goal. It was a sweet moment of validation when he got into the University of California, Berkeley, which was on his list of five! I am proud of both my sons and their single-minded quest towards getting into the best colleges for both their undergraduate and MBA degrees. The fact that I spent time with them and was able to mentor them played a big role. *So, find every excuse to bond with your children*; go hiking, take long walks or play games with them and become their trusted mentor. Even when my sons were studying in the US, I had told them that if they faced any serious problem of any kind, their first call should be to me. Yes, the calls came, but things worked out. I am so proud of my sons and our relationship.

Family Is the Centre of Your Universe

Our most important relationships are with spouse, children, parents and siblings.

One has to commit significant time, effort and resources to nurture these relationships to the best of one's ability and even at the cost of some other life goals.

I left my career at its peak in US to move to India to take care of my parents. Today, I consider it as one of my biggest achievements and source of fulfilment in life.

contd.

Balancing these relationships can be a challenge sometimes, but doing your unflinching best will go a long way in giving you satisfaction.

Relationships with children are special, a source of enormous pleasure and pride. We have to be a role model and mentor for our children.

'If you want to change the world, go home and love your family.'

—Mother Teresa

Relationships that I built during the course of my career have remained relevant and alive. Many people feel free to drop in for a chat or a word of advice. My door is always open. It's not just family, friends and co-workers that one needs to build meaningful relationships with. It's also community—your watchman, driver, or the underprivileged at large. They need your hand of friendship too. It could be just as simple as spotting that grandmother who sits by herself on that bench in your building. Walk up to her, sit down, talk. Tiny gestures like these cannot only spread so much joy in others, they will flood your own heart with a good measure of it!

'The quality of your life is the quality of your relationships.'

—Tony Robbins

What is the quality of your life?

Key Learnings

1. Relationships with family and friends are one of the greatest sources of happiness in life; they are vital to our well-being, and our mental and physical health.
2. You have to give your best as a husband, wife, son, daughter, sibling, father or mother. Poorly managed relationships can be the biggest source of regret in life, leading to stress, pain and unhappiness.
3. Networking in your professional field is critical to your long-term professional success.
4. There will be chunks of time periods when one goal overshadows your relationship goals. It's not a problem as long as you are cognizant of it and come back to relationship goals at the earliest.

Guru Mantra on Relationships from Prakash Padukone, ranked World Number One, Badminton, 1980

We are a close-knit family tied with strong relationships. We give a lot of importance to relationships, honesty and respect for parents and elders. We spent as much quality time with my daughters as possible, especially when they were younger. We would make it a point to have dinner together at the dining table to the extent it was possible. Now, whenever we meet, we talk transparently about our values, passions and dreams. As I always say, in the end, when your career is behind you, what remains with you and for you are relationships with family and friends.

MIND – BODY – SOUL

TEN

Mind–Body–Soul: The Key to Wellness

'Take care of your body. It's the only place you have to live in.'

—Jim Rohn

Greece, where the father of medicine, Hippocrates, invented and tested many medicinal breakthroughs, had a marvellous practice which the world is revisiting now. Whenever a person fell sick, three doctors would see a patient together. They were the 'knife' doctor, the 'herb' doctor, and the 'word' doctor. They knew that there is a connection between the mind, the body and the soul when it comes to wellness.

Your mind, body and soul are powerful 'significant others' to each other. If you abuse your body with substances and lack of exercise, the mind, too, falls ill. If you fill the mind with negative thoughts, your body takes the brunt. If your soul feels vacant and pointless, you wither away. It's all interconnected.

As a child, didn't we all enjoy playing, bouncing around, drawing with crayons, making sandcastles on the beach? When did we lose the ability to have pure fun without any agenda? Maybe, just growing up took its toll. So, for body–mind wellness, first 'relearn' how to have fun. *Fun is a great way to de-stress, forget your problems, boost your mood and reduce anxiety.* A nice side effect is that you build relationships and get to know people when you take part in fun group activities.

Since I am a strong proponent of a goal-based life, I suggest you convert your targeted fun activities into goals. You could play cricket or some other sport, you could go hiking, biking, jogging, take a long walk or learn to play a musical instrument. Cooking can not only be fun but is also a great diversion from the humdrum of life. Dancing can be a lot of fun. Studies have shown that dancing helps release mood-elevating chemicals in the brain, which can give you immediate relaxation. If you prefer a group activity, you could watch a concert with friends or just picnic with the family in the countryside!

Music is a magic bullet! Have you heard of the 'Mozart Effect'? According to some studies, listening to Mozart helped people improve spatial reasoning as measured by a sixteen-item test. Music can not only relax you, it can make you smarter!

It's a good idea to have a monthly goal to watch a movie with your loved ones. Goals for travel with your family are also a good idea. Once travel is chosen as a goal, you can save for a trip and make more efficient plans.

When you are having fun, your brain produces substances that can improve your health. These substances include endorphins, which are natural painkillers, and gamma globulin, which strengthens your immune system. *So, learn to have fun and be happy at all times!*

My Serious Fun Goals!

- Travelling—As a travel enthusiast, I have visited fifty-plus countries.
- Sports—As a sports lover, I have watched many world-class sports events.
- Music—As a music lover, I have been to hundreds of concerts featuring top artists in the world. Singing old songs and ghazals has been my hobby for a long time.
- Movies—I enjoy good movies.
- Food—As a foodie, I have tried cuisines of almost 100 countries.
- Reading—As an avid reader, not only have I read many books but I have also enjoyed interacting with many authors. In my home library, there is a section of books signed by authors.

Another aspect of holistic wellness is your physical health.

South of the main islands of Japan is a beautiful tropical paradise called Okinawa. People call it the healthiest place to be. A study conducted by the Okinawa Prefectural University's College of Nursing tells us that 82 per cent of individuals there are functioning independently at a mean age of ninety-two and almost two-thirds are functioning independently at a mean age of ninety-seven.

What is their secret? Well, one is diet. The local diet is rich in vegetables, soy products and seafood, with very little processed foods, reducing the environmental impact. Rich in flavonoids, carotenoids, vitamin E and lycopene from fruits, vegetables, legumes and proteins, this diet reduces the risk of heart disease, dementia and even some kinds of cancer. This, along with smaller meal portions, seems to be one of the most influential factors in the population's longevity.

Other than diet, Okinawans benefit from relationships. They live a physically active life with deep community bonds. Humans are social animals, and positive mental stimulation—being part of a larger community—also plays a huge role in overall good health.

Maintaining a healthy lifestyle is not easy, as all of us have experienced. But if one is clear on priorities, going jogging for thirty minutes instead of spending that time sitting at a bar with friends is a no-brainer. *Health goals can silently slide in priority unless you have a firm grip on them*. Work deadlines and travel can ambush you. But if you lose your health, how will you pursue other goals?

In addition to being physically active, make sure you don't ignore any warning signal that your body is sending: lethargy, an ache or any unusual discolouration or growth. Go for regular health check-ups. Stay away from cigarettes, vaping and drugs, and remain responsible about your alcohol consumption.

Keeping your mind in a positive state is also like an antidote to toxins. Meditation and mindfulness practices have a transformational impact on the brain, nervous system, endocrine system and hormones, which impact our mood, attention span and overall tranquillity. Even just a two-month disciplined practice of meditation can increase neurotransmitters like dopamine, serotonin and oxytocin that will make you happier and more productive.

Sample Health Goals

Exercise for thirty minutes a day seven days a week.
Or walk/jog thirty minutes a day three times a week.
Do yoga thirty minutes a day four times a week.
Do pranayama for thirty minutes three times a week.

---

contd.

> Eat a healthy breakfast every day.
> Eat dinner by 7 pm every day.
> Achieve ideal BMI and body weight by losing 5 kg
> in the next six months.
> Quit smoking.

Achieving meaningful success requires a number of things to line up, many that are in your control and have been discussed in this book earlier. But some are in the control of the Almighty and one needs his grace to make things happen.

> *'To enable one to attract god's grace, one needs prayer, service to others and living life based on a strong value system.'*
>
> —Dr Vivek Mansingh

Sometime in 2008, I felt a pain in my throat. I dismissed it as a case of seasonal flu. But it kept increasing. It was so excruciating that I couldn't swallow or talk. Even after some heavy-duty medicines, my situation was worsening. I went to see a doctor. He ran a few tests and said that it looked worrisome. He said that I needed cranial surgery. I consulted another doctor and he supported the earlier diagnosis and treatment. I remember that it was a Friday on which I got admitted for the surgery that was scheduled for the coming Monday. My family was devastated—they started praying fervently. My father, who was in Fatehpur, started a *Maha Mrityunjaya Jaap* in the temple he has built there—it is a chant for invoking god's powers to conquer death. Incredibly and without any medical explanation, an inner voice told me to not go for surgery. I walked out of the hospital. I saw another doctor, recommended by a dear friend, who diagnosed it as a case of thyroiditis. I was cured with a simple course of medication. *That is the grace of the supreme being and the power of prayers.*

Daily prayers reaffirm our faith in god and motivate us to go on the path of righteousness. Yoganandji in *The Autobiography of a Yogi* tells us to ask god to grant our wishes just like a child asks her father. I strongly suggest you should pray every day even for a few minutes and ask god to grant specific wishes. Other than attracting god's grace, you will embed a clear signal of your desires in your mind, resulting in more focus and motivation to work harder. Many times, I have asked my mentees that if god appeared before them and granted them three wishes, what would they ask for? Most people struggle to answer this, which suggests they do not know what they want! *So, if you don't know what you deeply desire, how will you create goals around achieving that?*

There is strong scientific evidence indicating that faith and prayer help us in experiencing greater physical, mental and psychological wellness. Did you know that brain activities in the frontal lobes change during prayer and meditation? These are the parts involved in motor function, problem solving, memory, language, judgement and social behaviour. Hence, you give your brain a beautiful experience when you pray!

In addition to praying, **identify the values that you stand for**. Articulate them and talk about them as often as you can. For example, while having dinner with your family or friends, talk about, say, a simple value such as honesty or integrity or generosity and how you have lived that value with examples and stories. Your values guide your decisions and set the tone for how you live your life. **When we live by our values, they are the GPS or Google Map that guides us in everything we do**. They give our lives both direction and meaning and build strong character, which becomes a platform from which we jump to achieve other life goals. The first step is to identify your core values and write them down—integrity, kindness, compassion, gratitude, forgiveness, respect, generosity—whatever defines you. You can make a charter of values for the whole family as well. Then, live these values without any compromise. Living your values brings stability and authenticity to your life, because people know who you are and what you stand for (or won't stand for). Your leadership ability, relationships and respect will increase.

You can set goals in the area of oneness with the supreme being. These goals can be daily prayers, meditating thirty minutes a day, attending a course on holistic wellness, living with integrity, respect and generosity as family values, visiting a holy place of your choice and so on.

> **Examples of My Spiritual Goals**
>
> Have deep faith in god, ask for the grace and blessings of god.
>
> With that goal in mind, I have participated in many spiritual activities including pujas and visits to temples, gurudwaras, mazārs (shrines) and churches, and studying our scriptures.
>
> I have done courses of Yoganandji, Sri Sri Ravi Shankar and Sri Sadhguru Ji.
>
> These spiritual activities have given me tremendous courage during difficult times and overall success in life.
>
> My family values are integrity, kindness, gratitude and generosity.
>
> I am working on my goal of practising meditation for thirty minutes a day. Even being keenly aware that I am missing it and struggling is a good starting point!

Be at the centre of the life you are building. Chase a butterfly. Lie on the beach. Pray. Smell the roses. Laugh like a child. Steal a moment to be with your loved one. Always keep yourself nourished! When we are happy and positive, we work smarter, get more motivated and are more likely to achieve our goals. So, be happy!

Key Learnings

1. Work hard, play hard. Having fun is important.
2. Take care of your body, mind and soul. It is the undeniable platform one needs to propel oneself from, to achieve anything and everything in life.
3. To attract the grace of the Almighty, one needs prayers, service to others and living a life based on a strong value system.

Guru Mantra from Sadhguru Ji, spiritual leader, founder, Isha Foundation

Yoga is capable of activating inner energies in a way that your body and mind function at their optimal capacity. It is a means to create inner situations exactly the way you want them. All human beings, without exception, are capable of turning into the architects of their own joy and the masters of their own destiny. Yoga offers us the key.

Guru Mantra from John Chambers, chairman and CEO, Cisco

I took Cisco from $1 billion in revenue to $47 billion during my tenure as a CEO. I had a lot of ups and downs, but I never missed my morning jog, family priorities or fishing expeditions.

Guru Mantra from Dr Devi Shetty, cardiac surgeon and founder, Narayana Health

Let's say we are in a stormy sea alone in a boat, trying desperately to direct it to the shore using the rudder. We are clinging to that lever, trying to guide the boat in adverse conditions. Somehow, and after a big struggle, we manage to reach the shore. We are so relieved and also proud of our steering skills. But we must realize that only a small rudder was in our hand! So, acknowledging the role of the Almighty in life is important.

GIVING BACK

ELEVEN

Giving Back: Creating Meaning in Life

'To move forward, you have to give back.'
—Oprah Winfrey

Happiness is an unlimited resource. You can create huge amounts of it out of virtually nothing. And the astonishing thing is that when you do something to create happiness for others, you create it for yourself, too. Yes, research shows that the pleasure centres of the brain of a person who gives back to the community are always activated! To create meaning in our lives, we need to think beyond ourselves and about how we can help others. *Giving back means doing good for others while not expecting anything in return.* Recognize that if you can buy this book and read this message, you are privileged. Recognize that your privilege comes largely from the circumstances you were born into. As part of this privilege, it is your duty to give back. **Giving back helps you stay grounded in your journey to** *meaningful success and can add a deep sense of purpose to your life.*

Giving back will also make you feel deeply fulfilled. Your biggest reward in giving back is the realization that you've made a significant change in someone's life. You will earn respect in your own eyes and also from others. *So, while I love my late parents, I respect them more for what they did for others than for what they did for us.*

Adding Years to Life and Fulfilment with Giving Back

After my mother passed away in 2003, it was extremely hard on my seventy-six-year-old father. He was sad and had lost his sense of purpose.

Although he had always been charitable and generous, my brother and I encouraged him to revamp his efforts in a structured manner. He took on the cause of getting corrective surgeries done for differently abled children in Fatehpur, his birthplace and the city where he lived all his life. He partnered with Narayan Seva Sansthan in Udaipur, and would send the children and their families there from Fatehpur, to get the surgeries done at no charge to them. He got so passionately engaged in it that he would be thinking about these children all the time and taking calls from their

contd.

parents 24/7. Over the years, he facilitated surgeries for 300 children who, thanks to him, walked for the first time in their lives!

He also reconstructed a Shiva temple in Fatehpur. He was so passionate that he would oversee the reconstruction himself and be physically present for eight to ten hours a day in the bone-chilling winters and sweltering summers for five years!

This experience of giving back gave him new enthusiasm and purpose to live, and he lived well and happily for the next fifteen years and passed away in 2018 with a feeling of fulfilment.

The universal law of giving says that the more you give, the more you will receive. Even a simple act of donating blood has been found to create happiness for people who did so as compared to a group who didn't.

Tristen Inagaki and Naomi Eisenberger from the University of Pittsburgh concluded after a series of MRIs, that an act of giving can stimulate portions of the brain that reduce stress and make you feel better.

The very first person to reach the status of 'billionaire' was a man who knew how to set goals and follow through. At the age of twenty-three, he had become a millionaire, and by the age of fifty, a billionaire. There was only one issue: all his goals were around creating wealth and accumulating power.

But three years later, at the age of fifty-three, he fell gravely sick. His hair fell in clumps and he was tormented with the most excruciating body pain. While he had the money to buy anything, all he could eat was a sick man's diet. He could barely sleep, wouldn't smile, and nothing in life meant anything to him. His doctors gave him less than a year to live. The newspapers had prepared his obituary. The man who could control the business world suddenly realized he wasn't in control of his own life, and that death was the only certainty in life.

One morning, he woke up after a fitful sleep during which he had a vision. While he couldn't remember the details, he recollected the message: that he couldn't take any of his riches and successes with him into the next world.

He summoned his team and made a declaration—that he wanted to donate extensively to hospitals, research and mission work. On that day, John D. Rockefeller established his now famous foundation, which was instrumental in the discovery of penicillin and cures for current strains of malaria, tuberculosis and diphtheria. The benefits that have accrued from his decision are many, but perhaps the most spectacular part of Rockefeller's story is that the moment he began to live generously, his body's chemistry was altered so significantly that he recovered from his illness. It seemed that he would die at the age of fifty-three, but he lived to be ninety-eight! *There is such power in generosity and giving back.*

I strongly believe in giving back. My goal in 2000 was to serve on the board of a reputable NGO. I started working as a volunteer at Janaagraha, one of the best and most impactful NGOs of India. Later, around 2008, I joined the board to assist in its mission to improve urban living across India. I have great regard for my alma mater, NIT Allahabad, and wanted to do something for the institution. I gifted 500 books to the library and served on the board of NIT Allahabad for five years. I would consider giving back, even in tiny ways, one of my biggest and most satisfying achievements in life.

Examples of My Giving-Back Goals at Retirement

(At age sixty, for the next ten years. Hope it inspires many sixty-year-olds.)

1. Mentor 1000+ people face to face (from CEOs to the driver's or domestic help's children).
2. Write a book, and through the book and its associated website, mentor 1 million young people.
3. Help create 3 billion-dollar start-ups in India.
4. Help create 50,000 jobs.
5. Help 1,00,000 less privileged people through Fatehpur General Hospital and ICU.

contd.

6. Establish an eye hospital in Fatehpur for the less privileged.

7. Impact 10 lakh children through indirect intervention at Janaagraha and other NGOs.

8. In addition, my other giving-back goals include paying fair wages to my house help, educating their children and supporting a number of charities, including a free medicine programme and a school for handicapped children in Fatehpur.

9. I strongly encourage everyone to do something for your village, town or city, and your school or college. It is these that gave you a platform to succeed.

The gifts of caring, compassion and appreciation are invaluable ones that do not cost you anything. Do not wait to give when you have a lot; instead, give what you can, whenever you can. My children would give away a portion of their pocket money when they were younger; their birthdays were first celebrated at blind schools. During their student life, they volunteered for various causes and taught the children of our staff. Ayush's way of celebrating our birthdays and anniversaries is by gifting to a charity and sharing the gift certificate with us. My teams at Dell and Cisco volunteered extensively. If you can read this book, you can at least teach reading to an underprivileged child for an hour a week. *Stay committed to giving, NOT 1 per cent of time and money, but something significant in your lifetime.*

The causes to support are plenty. Pick something that resonates with you, something that tugs at your heartstrings. Once you have identified an area, go ahead and write down specifics of what you will do. It's never too late to begin! But don't wait!

Here are some examples of giving-back goals to help you get the ball rolling:

- I will vote. Even if it means choosing the NOTA button.
- I will support local businesses.
- I will provide jobs to those in need and give fair wages.
- I will pay for the education of my driver's or domestic help's children.
- I will teach my house help's daughter or son for thirty minutes every day.
- I will mentor children in my community.
- I will serve as a volunteer for <name> organization for 100 hours this year.
- I will donate Rs 10,000 to Akshayapatra or some other NGO this year.

contd.

- I will invest in companies that are uplifting the community, not those causing harm.
- I will start an NGO for the education of the underprivileged.
- I will build a hospital or school in my village.

Key Learnings

1. To create meaning in our life, we need to think beyond ourselves and help others.
2. Giving back helps us stay grounded, adds purpose and provides a great sense of fulfilment.
3. Pick a cause that resonates with you and start engaging NOW with whatever you can do.
4. Do not wait for when you have a lot of money; you can always give time, advice or any such help.

Guru Mantra on Giving Back from Narayana Murthy, founder, Infosys

My father was a high-school teacher. We were eight children; my paternal grandmother stayed with us. Therefore, there were eleven mouths to feed on the salary of a high-school teacher. Still, my mother made sure that, at every dinner, we hosted a child from a less fortunate family. So, we had seven children come and eat with us seven days of the week. Despite the fact that we were poor, my mother wanted to share whatever little we had with the child of someone who was earning even less than what my father was earning.

Guru Mantra on Giving Back from Ramesh and Swati Ramanathan, founders, Janaagraha

If there is a voice in your head telling you to do something for the larger good, listen to it. Don't be afraid of your parents or social circle frowning upon your plans. Believe that your contributions are rich, necessary, different and needed. Great societies are made by average people solving public problems and adding value. Even if you give one hour a week, it's wonderful. But start right away; give time, money or whatever you can.

Guru Mantra on Giving Back from Vinita Bali, ex-CEO, Britannia

Look at your life as the opportunity to change things not just for yourself but also for your family, society and planet. Whatever your sphere of influence. Don't be afraid to lead or follow, as long as you are driving positive change.

Mentee Speaks: Kavitha Sai, leader at Microsoft India

Dr Vivek has played a key role as a mentor in my career journey. It is rare that one comes across a reporting leader who invests in you as a mentor. Destiny bestowed him upon me as my manager and, looking back, it was truly a blessing!

Apart from learning about leadership, management, innovation and excellence that have served me extremely well in my profession over the years, I learnt the significance of giving back. I have chosen to support the causes of autism and an institution, Women in Profession. It has made my life amazingly fulfilling and enriching.

LEARN FROM THE BEST

SUCCESS LEAVES CLUES

TWELVE

Success Bites from the Super Successful

'As you stride towards your goals, keep looking for clues of success left by the people you admire.'
—Dr Vivek Mansingh

The master was seated on the roots of an ancient tree, lit by light filtering through the mesh of foliage above. A melody of silence and the deep aroma of the forest's wood permeated the area. Students filed in, knowing that their training was going to equip them for a life full of meaningful success. They were anxious to get the maximum benefit from it.

One student approached the master and asked how he could maximize the benefits accruing from the training. 'Think of me as a fountain of holy water,' the master explained. 'You can come to me with a teaspoon, or a cup, or a barrel. It is up to you how much you want to drink.'

The masters are there. It is how much we gather from the outpouring of their wisdom; with craving, openness and persistence.

Through exclusive interviews for this book, I have tapped into the brilliant minds of some distinguished masters whom I admire. These people share three Padma Vibhushans, five Padma Bhushans and four Padma Shree awards among themselves for service to the nation. These esteemed people are Narayana Murthy, Ratan Tata, Sadhguru Ji, Kiran Mazumdar-Shaw, Dr Devi Shetty, John Chambers, Rahul Dravid, Prakash Padukone, Vinita Bali, Vani Kola, and Ramesh and Swati Ramanathan. *All of them have achieved amazing success by passionately pursuing their goal-based journeys along the lines of ideas shared in the book*. Their presence in my life's journey has been enormously inspirational, and here, I attempt to bring a generous serving of that inspiration to you, too.

The videos of these interviews are available at www. vivekmansingh.com.

Narayana Murthy on Leadership and Success

The iconic founder of Infosys has been described as the 'father of the Indian IT sector' by *Time* magazine for his contribution to outsourcing in India. Infosys currently has a revenue of $12 billion a year and employs close to 2,50,000 people.

He has received a Légion d'honneur from France, a CBE from Britain and a Padma Vibhushan and Padma Shri from India. In 2014, Murthy was ranked thirteenth among CNBC's 25 global business leaders and listed among the '12 greatest entrepreneurs of our time' by *Fortune* in 2012. *The Economist* ranked him among the ten most-admired global business leaders in 2005.

Currently, Murthy serves on the boards of many foundations and well-known universities in the US, including Cornell University, Wharton School, the Graduate School of Business at Stanford University and the Rhodes Trust at Oxford.

He is also a trustee of the Infosys Science Foundation, which governs the Infosys Prize, an annual award to honour outstanding achievements of researchers and scientists.

I have spent some illuminating moments with Murthy during my Dell and Cisco days, and during many events of Janaagraha (the NGO, on whose board I serve, which is also supported by Murthy). He is one of the persons I admire the most and highly recommend his books including *A Better India: A Better World*. He is also a big inspiration for my son Ayush since his high-school days when he interviewed Murthy for a project as a young student. A person in whose presence I am always humbled and invigorated.

VM: What, according to you, are the top three factors that led to your success?

NM: First of all, luck and the blessings of my elders, such as my parents and teachers. A lot of friends during my student days, and later as well, who were much smarter than I was, did not succeed to the extent that I seem to have done. As Louis Pasteur said, 'When God is shy to announce his presence, he comes in the form of chance.' There were so many occasions when what Infosys offered to the client wasn't as good as what the competitors offered, yet we won the deal. Therefore, I have always believed that god's blessings and those of elders are important.

Secondly, I have always believed in leading by example and showing the path to my younger colleagues by living it. The salaries of all the founders were the same till we retired even though some of them were a lot younger and less experienced than I was. I started that trend by taking a smaller pay raise than my subordinates and brought that practice to Infosys. I took it upon myself to lead by example. When I wanted Infoscions to come to the office on time, I came to the office at 6.20

a.m. and then others would automatically come in by 7.45 a.m. I did not have to tell them.

Third is the extraordinary value system that my co-founders exhibited right from the first day. To every one of them, earning the respect of society mattered the most. Their aspirations were high, and their objective in everything they did was to become more and more respectable. They accepted total austerity, deferred gratification, were committed to teamwork, showed full commitment to Infosys and to my leadership. They brought with them complementary skills like selling, technology, HR, finance and communication.

VM: Would you call yourself a goal-driven person? How did goals play a part in your life?

NM: I was a leftist when I was a student and I believed in Nehruvian socialism. I believed in the state playing a big role in development. While I was a reasonably good student in my undergraduate studies in Mysore, I wasn't very focused. I did not have clear goals even at IIT Kanpur, where I did my graduate studies. However, when I worked in Paris during the early 1970s, I spent a lot of time observing how Western societies had developed. I read a lot about socialism, communism and capitalism. I met leaders of these -isms in Paris. I travelled a lot in Western Europe. That was when I realized that the only way that India could solve the problem of poverty was by creating lots and lots of jobs with good income. I understood that entrepreneurship was the only mechanism to make it happen. An incident while I was hitchhiking converted me from a confused leftist to a determined capitalist. So, I became very goal-oriented when I returned to India in the mid-'70s.

VM: You have achieved amazing success. What legacy would you like to leave?

NM: I am not sure that I can claim to have been successful in any aspect of my life. However, there are lots of good values that I try to practise every day. I am sure that there would have been times when I failed in living up to my revered values, but I continue to strive to become better in integrity, fairness, generosity, transparency, accountability, starting every transaction on a zero base, leadership by example and excellence in everything I do. I am often asked how I would like to be remembered. I answer that I want to be remembered as a fair person who practises the golden rule: do unto others what you want them to do unto you.

VM: What specific actions did you take to work towards excellence for yourself and Infosys?

NM: Excellence is, I agree, competing with yourself on a daily basis to become better and better each day in every action of yours. This is the ultimate challenge!

For Infosys, I did it by asking if I was doing things faster today, cheaper today and better today than I was yesterday. It requires one to create an environment around you that is open to new ideas from others, respect for youth, meritocracy, fairness, a hierarchy of ideas, justice, speed and imagination.

These, I believe, are extremely important, particularly in India, since we are the most egoistic people in the world. Age is the determining factor in India in decisions. Apathy is our staple diet. Our favourite phrase is '*chalta hai*'. And time has no value for us. Therefore, adhering to these values could make you unpopular. I would urge everyone seeking excellence to persist despite an unfavourable environment around you.

VM: Do share some examples of how thinking out of the box has helped you and Infosys.

NM: At Infosys, we innovated the global delivery model (where work could be done from anywhere in the world) and the twenty-four-hour day (by using teams across the world in different time zones). These have become globally accepted as important tools in the software services industry. In India, we achieved many firsts like a listing on Nasdaq, first in large-scale employee stock option plans, first to achieve Capability Maturity Model (CMM) levels 4 and 5, first leadership institute in the country, and the first software company with a large campus. In other words, we have done a lot of things in innovation. But I believe that innovation, Vivek, as you pointed out, is the formal word for thinking outside the box.

I believe that innovation should not be the prerogative of a few seniors in the organization, but it must be the mantra of everybody from the janitor to the CEO. There must be opportunity for everybody to improve processes. After all, Peter Drucker said, 'Innovation is change that creates a new dimension of performance.' So, only when innovation is owned by every employee in the company, and every employee asks this question: how do I do things faster, cheaper and better than yesterday, that an organization becomes strong.

VM: What are your thoughts on leadership?

NM: I think leadership is never given, it is always taken. In every situation, where there are many people in a group, some evolve to be leaders. An experiment was conducted in a section of US universities where they put a set of high achievers from various fields—sports, business, academia, politics—together in a house. Quite automatically after a few days, natural groups formed and leaders emerged entirely on their own!

A leader is a transformative agent. Transformation, as you know, is a big-ticket change. Leadership can be described by the late Robert Kennedy's words (who borrowed them from G.B. Shaw). He said, 'Most people see things as they are and wonder why, but I dream of things as they are not and then say, why not?' That, to me, is the best example of leadership. The first attribute of a great leader, therefore, is high aspiration. Aspirations build civilizations.

Secondly, a good leader has the ability to raise the courage, confidence, energy and enthusiasm of a set of ordinary people to do extraordinary things and to achieve the impossible.

The third attribute is the capacity to earn the trust of one's followers through leadership by example, by walking the talk and practising the precept.

VM: *What would be your 'leadership mantra' for the youth of India?*

NM: The problems in India today are immense and no individual can solve them alone. We need teams that have high competence, enthusiasm and energy, and are ready to work hard together.

The leaders we need are those who will be adept at bringing together such teams and welding them together as a unified entity. The teams need to be indefatigable, trustworthy, complementary in skills, harmonious, rejoicing in the success of others, ready to do what seems impossible and disciplined.

Without such leadership, you cannot drive a significant mass to change India. Our country needs lots of teams to work hard to solve problems, and therefore there is considerable opportunity for our youngsters to show leadership. It's for them to take on the challenge.

VM: What has been the role of mentors and role models in your life?

NM: Role models are extremely important to bring confidence and drive one to success in difficult tasks that face our young leaders. They demonstrate sacrifice, hard work, selflessness, courage, competence, aspirations, discipline, excellence, fairness, justice, transparency and accountability, putting the interests of the institution ahead of one's own personal interests. Role models show us that these seemingly unattainable capabilities can, in fact, be practised. I have been fortunate to have had several such role models who have shaped me. My parents taught me values like honesty, hard work, generosity, sharing, teamwork, concern for the less fortunate ones and high aspirations.

My high school and college teachers taught me about putting the interests of the community ahead of one's personal interests, starting every transaction on a zero base and being patriotic.

My boss in Paris taught me the importance of bottom line responsibility and accountability. Therefore, I am the product of whatever I have learnt from these people.

I have been fortunate to have many mentors in the form of parents, teachers and bosses. While building Infosys, I learnt certain things from Microsoft, human and corporate culture values from HP when Bill and David were running the show, consistency in top line and bottom line growth from GE, and focus on quality from

Motorola. In other words, we learn different attributes from different organizations and individuals.

VM: How have you managed your personal relationships and professional duties?

NM: I have been very fortunate that I have never ever put the interests of my family ahead of my company's interests or my values. I am very grateful to my wife and children for helping me do this. I kept my relationship with my family so clear that when my children came to Infosys and wanted to eat at the canteen, they paid for their lunch. This is something I am very proud of.

VM: 'Giving back' is a source of fulfilment and happiness. When did you first start; what was your inspiration then and now?

NM: Giving back to society has been at least a 2000-year-old practice in India. My father was a high-school teacher. We were eight children, my paternal grandmother stayed with us. Therefore, there were eleven mouths to feed on the salary of a high-school teacher. Still, my mother made sure that, at every dinner, we hosted a child from a less fortunate family. So, we had seven children come and eat with us seven days of the week. Despite the fact that we were poor, my mother wanted to share whatever little we had with the child of someone who was earning even less than what my father was earning.

My parents and my in-laws have taught us that bringing a smile on the face of a less fortunate person is the definition of success.

Overall, higher-level education and ground-level growth are very important for this country and these are the two things that our family has focused on in our approach to giving back.

VM: What is your overall message for the youth of India?

NM: We are living in an extraordinary time in the history of our country. For the first time in the last 200 years, the world expects India to contribute significantly in the global bazaar on issues like climate change, sustainability and making the life of the poor on this planet better. To do this, India must first become strong, economically and socially. We must have peace, harmony, health, education, nutrition and shelter for every Indian belonging to every religion, socio-economic status, region and accomplishment. Such a task requires high aspirations, discipline, hard work, honesty, teamwork and rising above personal ideologies and interests.

I want every single youngster to remember that they have this opportunity to make India a better place. I did not have this opportunity when I was young, so I want every youngster to remember and achieve this plausible and noble goal.

Ratan Tata on Leadership and Start-ups

Under Ratan Tata's chairmanship, various group companies of Tata Sons went through massive growth as he turned the salt-to-software conglomerate into a $100 billion group. He also steered the conglomerate's overseas expansion as various Tata Group companies acquired large global brands like Tetley, Corus and Jaguar Land Rover. He launched his dream project, the Nano, at the Auto Expo in 2008. Dubbed as the most affordable car, Nano took Tata Motors to the world stage, making it a case study in many business schools.

Awarded with a Padma Vibhushan in 2008, this doyen of Indian business has a number of prestigious awards to his name, including the Carnegie Medal of Philanthropy, the International Distinguished Achievement Award (2005), Business Leader of the Year (2010—the Asian Awards) and Transformational Leader of the Decade (2013).

He studied architecture and structural engineering at New York's Cornell University and later he joined the Tata Group. After completing fifty glorious years in the Tata Group, he retired and shifted focus to mentoring and investing in start-ups. He also continues to be involved with the Tata Trust, the charitable organization of the Tata Group founders, which focuses on tackling child malnutrition, healthcare, literacy and social justice.

Ratan Tata speaks in measured words, and each word is gold. Such is the wisdom of this great man. He is one of my most admired global leaders; I hope he inspires you as much as he inspires me.

VM: Mr Tata, your leadership has seen the phenomenal rise of the Tata Group and you have had amazing success. What were some basic principles that you based your decisions on while building the Tata Group?

RT: Decisions were based on the situation at that time. I have always tried to do the right thing even if that wasn't the easiest choice, whether it was related to manpower or shutting down a business. My guiding principle is that one should be able to sleep at night without wondering if he's done something wrong.

VM: Looking back, starting from 1971, when you turned around National Radio Electronics, restructured some of the Tata Group companies, acquired Tetley, Jaguar Land Rover, Corus and then launched Nano, what led you to take such high-risk and game-changing decisions?

RT: Again, each decision should be seen through the lens of the situation at that time. When I look back at, say, Jaguar Land Rover, it started as clandestine meetings with the Ford Motor Company that wanted to shed this weight around its neck. I thought I was being made the sacrificial goat; what was I going to do with a failed car company that an institution like Ford had not been able to turn around? I was very interested in Land Rover because we made SUVs but was not interested in having to deal with Jaguar. But Ford refused to separate the two so we just took the whole company. I remember the first town hall in their factory and facing an onslaught of questions that had been fuelled by so many rumours. I said, 'Let's work shoulder to shoulder and restore the glory to these brands.' Believe it or not, the people of Jaguar Land Rover did just that and completely on their own! They rose to the occasion. If you go back there today, it's a different company as we were able to motivate the people.

In the case of the Nano, it was a dream of mine. Whenever I would see families of four or five on a scooter, I would dream about making it safer for them. I am quite a doodler, particularly when board meetings are boring! I would often doodle ideas on how to make a scooter safer. That led to a doodle of a small family car that would increase safety and shield the family from rain and such. Then, we had to move the factory. And, we also became rather complacent and made many mistakes. With all these challenges, though Nano may not have had a great ride, I feel it's still an excellent product in the Rs 1 lakh car market.

We displayed the car at the Geneva motor show and noticed Japanese and Korean visitors taking measuring tapes and inspecting the car. I thought, 'Oh! We really caught their attention!'

VM: Any advice on learning from the integration of companies?

RT: I think one thing that is necessary is the motivation of the people and their belief that they can achieve success. This applies to companies of all sizes. There needs to be a sense of pride in the company they belong to. This is easier in a start-up than a bigger company but it's a fundamental requirement for all companies.

VM: What made you interested in start-ups after retirement?

RT: It was partly by accident. In the years I was with the Tata Group, I always looked at the start-up sector as exciting. I was always attracted to youngsters who had the motivation to start something new. But when I was with the Tata Group, it could have been a conflict of interest. After retirement, I have the liberty to support these young people with token investments and guidance.

VM: Are Indian start-ups disruptive enough?

RT: I don't think we have as many disruptive start-ups in India as there may be in other countries. Perhaps it is because there isn't enough support in the environment.

Maybe we have a protectionist instinct and want to work with what we already have.

VM: Any learnings from your engagement with start-ups?

RT: I have realized that I may not be the right person to give advice since I am still learning. I am watching how businesses that look completely undoable to me become great successes and some that appear to start as a great idea just don't make it. It all goes back to the people, to the founders, their motivation and the conviction they carry.

VM: Most of your investments are in the consumer internet space. Was there any reason for that?

RT: India is such a big country with such a large consumer base and the new trends of e-commerce and marketing have opened Indians to goods and services they didn't have before. So, to me, this was an enormous change happening in India and I wanted to be part of it.

VM: Any sectors that in your view are going to be big?

RT: On the technology side, many breakthroughs are happening, so there are many sectors where exciting things are happening. But one that I am most excited about is medical research. I think India is poised to play a big role in some of the medical discoveries. In the ten years that lie ahead of us, we may well see diseases that were considered terminal becoming treatable, and much of the work would be done in India since the entry cost is not that high and the needed skills are there. We will play a big role in some of the discoveries. It could start collaboratively but India will be the centre of bio and medical sciences in the future. In the online space, manufacturing and many other areas, there are better ways of doing something and opportunities are great for start-ups.

VM: India has done pretty well in the software services business for many years with many companies having revenues above $10 billion and market caps above $20 billion. What is the future of software products in your view?

RT: I think the future is going to lie in algorithms that would be self-programming and centred around artificial intelligence, which are, in a manner of speaking, all software products. They will, in many ways, replace human inputs. For example, autonomous cars, which are end products of a series of software products in artificial intelligence and pattern recognition. With proper innovation in these exciting areas, India will have a bright future in the software products space.

VM: In India, 1 million young people are joining the workforce every month, while automation is being adopted across industries. How does the country deal with this conflict: providing jobs versus rapid automation?

RT: I think India has a tremendous requirement of infrastructure in massive public works that can employ tens of thousands of people across the country. That's one bucket of employment. The other is technology-dependent areas of work that can employ young people with technical skills and this bucket can grow if we keep creating high-technology enterprises. Somewhere, it will come together at a later point in time, complementing each other.

VM: What's your view on the government getting involved in helping create a good start-up ecosystem?

RT: It's hard for me to say. Government organizations like DARPA in the US have been putting billions of dollars in their companies. NASA has done the same in space. But, yes, I do see a role for the government; they could and should play a role provided they embody the entrepreneurial spirit that is necessary.

VM: Will future Googles come out of India?

RT: Well, if two smart people from Stanford could make a search engine there, I don't see why it couldn't happen in India. If we can create the right environment where we applaud people rather than hold them back; if we remove roadblocks for the young people who have the entrepreneurial spirit and have investors support their start-ups, it will happen here too.

VM: Have you noticed the quality of start-ups improving day by day?

RT: Yes, certainly. There are more start-ups, the magnitude and scales are bigger, and the knowledge base has grown too.

VM: Your thoughts on the future of start-ups in India?

RT: More big companies will recognize that there are better ways of doing something. I foresee more momentum in start-ups doing things in a more cost-effective way and with greater capabilities. India will be more energized and flourish more with the start-up sector doing well. The excitement of being in the new area and participating in something that has not been done before is something to look forward to. I wish this sector all success!

VM: What would be your advice to entrepreneurs?

RT: More than ability, I have valued the attitude, maturity and seriousness of founders. That meant more to me than any other single factor. Fire in the belly is needed, inventing a better way to do something is important, as is being particular about not going ahead if there are ethical issues, and finally, having the courage and tenacity to see it through.

Sadhguru Ji on Mind, Body and Soul

Sadhguru Ji, often known as the 'Millennial Guru', is famous worldwide for founding the Isha Foundation, a spiritual organization focusing on yoga and social work. For his passion for teaching yoga and holistic living, he is revered by millions across the world. He is much-loved for his hard-hitting, highly-relatable sermons that are packed with much humour and laughter! With his unique and incisive vision, he speaks eloquently about the need to be deeply aware of one's self and being meditative right from a young age.

He has written several books, such as *Inner Engineering: A Yogi's Guide to Joy*, *Mystic's Musings* and *Death: An Inside Story*. His book *Karma: A Yogi's Guide to Crafting Your Destiny* made the *New York Times* bestsellers list. It was a moment of pride for all Indians when he addressed the United Nations Millennium World Peace Summit, the British Parliament's House of Lords, Massachusetts Institute of Technology and International Institute for Management Development. He has also spoken at the annual World Economic Forum in 2007, 2017 and 2020.

In 2017, he received the Padma Vibhushan from the Government of India for his contributions to social welfare.

'As long as you are locked up in your own logic, the magic of life will not reveal itself to you,' he says.

I have personally benefitted from his Inner Engineering course and my face-to-face, one-to-one meeting with him. He is one of the most impressive persons I have ever met. Here are his thoughts on taking care of mind, body and soul, and leadership.

VM: You have interacted with many top business and political leaders. In your opinion, what are the top three qualities of these leaders?

Sadhguru: A leader is someone who has deep insights. In other words, he sees what others are not able to see. A leader must also be a symbol of integrity and must be able to inspire the best in those around him. Being an inspiration need not necessarily mean that a leader has to be very charismatic or flamboyant. Many inspire others simply out of their absolute commitment to what they do. So these are the three 'I's: Insight, Integrity, and Inspiration.

VM: My definition of leadership is: 'The ability to motivate yourself and your team towards achieving a goal, and getting the best out of you and your team, even in adverse circumstances.' Your thoughts on leadership?

Sadhguru: If you are a leader, you need to do everything that works in the best interest of everyone, or at least as many people as possible. You have to be inclusive—every thought, every emotion, every action that you perform should not be about you but others and your followers. Consider everyone's well-being.

VM: To achieve success, one has to make sure mind, body and soul are taken care of. Your thoughts on the best way for people to do it?

Sadhguru: In yoga, we look at the human body as five *koshas* or sheaths. The first sheath is called *annamaya kosha* or the food body, because what you call the physical body is just a heap of food. The second sheath is called *manomaya kosha* or the mental body. These two layers can only function in connection with the third dimension, the energy body or *pranamaya kosha*. You can compare this to computers today—there is hardware and software, but by themselves they cannot do anything unless you plug the computer into quality power.

Pranamaya kosha is the dimension in which most of the yogic practices function. If you keep your pranamaya kosha in perfect balance and fully activated, you will be in a great mental and physical state and there can be no such thing as disease either in your physical or mental body.

Yoga is capable of activating inner energies in a way that your body and mind function at their optimal capacity. It is a means to create inner situations exactly the way you want them. When it comes to external situations, we are all differently capable. But when it comes to the inner situation, we are all equally capable. All human beings, without exception, are capable of turning into the architects of their own joy and the masters of their own destiny. Yoga offers us the key.

VM: One has to aspire big to achieve big goals. So, how does one create a balance between being aspirational and being content?

Sadhguru: Contentment means containment. Why would anyone want to contain his life? If you have lived a life of contentment, that means you did not live, you contained your life.

It is very natural for every human being to strive to be something more than what he or she is right now. The problem with our world is that there is not too much ambition, but too little. We have scaled down our ambitions. We need to up the stakes. Why are you stingy about your desires? Anyway, you want well-being, so why don't you be magnanimous? It is not just about, 'I want to be well.' It is 'I want the whole world to be well. I want the whole existence to be well. I want all life to be well.' Be really greedy with your ambitions. Whatever is your ambition for yourself, extend that to all life on this planet. Make your greed limitless, your ambition boundless, and watch your inner genius flower.

If we bring about this shift in leaders, from operating out of narrow personal ambitions to operating out of a larger vision, that will be the greatest thing for the future generations of the world.

VM: A short message to our youth about doing well for themselves and the world.

Sadhguru: Youth means a lot of energy. In terms of energy, what a youth can do, a child or an old man cannot do. But unbridled energy without stability and direction is always destructive. Whether they are in academics, vocational training, or simply doing whatever they wish to in their lives, if only youth are a little more stable, this energy could be put to better use for their own and everyone's well-being.

Youthfulness will go waste if there is no stability. Only those who are stable can use the quality and the talent that they have to the fullest extent. The most important thing that needs to happen to youth on the planet is to become meditative. Before the youth manage businesses, nations and the world, it is extremely important that they learn to manage themselves.

The whole process of yoga is the science of inner management where you create an inner possibility of being blissful, joyful, peaceful by your own nature, not because of something that happens around you. So, yoga shows the path on which you can build your life and achieve success.

Kiran Mazumdar-Shaw on Leadership and Success

Dr Kiran Mazumdar-Shaw, a pioneer of the biotechnology industry in India, is the chairperson and managing director of Biocon, India's leading biopharmaceutical company. One of *Time* magazine's 100 most influential people in the world, she has led Biocon to become a global biopharmaceutical enterprise committed to reducing therapy costs of chronic conditions like diabetes, cancer and autoimmune diseases.

She is the recipient of several awards, the most noteworthy being the Padma Bhushan and Padma Shri. The US-based Chemical Heritage Foundation conferred her with the 2014 Othmer Gold Medal and Germany-based Kiel Institute for the World Economy awarded her its coveted 2014 Global Economy Prize for Business.

Her philanthropic initiative, the Mazumdar Shaw Medical Centre, aims to create a sustainable, affordable cancer-care model. She is an independent member of the board of Infosys and has also been the chair of the board of governors of the Indian Institute of Management Bangalore.

I have admired Kiran for her passion and focus on solving difficult medical problems of a global scale. Here, I wish to bring her inspirational thoughts to all, especially women.

VM: You have been immensely successful, Kiran. What was your inspiration?

KM: I drew inspiration from a compelling sense of self-interest to make India a better country. I wanted my country and my immediate community to be more advanced. As a young student in India, I had observed a lot of brain drain. Good professionals were leaving. I felt, why can't we create better career options in our country?

Inspiration comes in many ways. It can be people who inspire you or a problem that concerns or worries you.

Biological science was my passion. I was inspired by the fact that tiny microbes, such as bacteria and yeast, could be life-saving. That fuelled an interest in brewing. My late father said that if I was interested in learning what yeast could do, I should study brewing. I did that but when I came back to India, I noticed that the brewing industry was too conservative to embrace a woman.

That led me to start my own biotech company. It was about enzyme technology. I could use the same knowledge here in a meaningful way. We started replacing chemical processes within enzyme processes. It was an eco-friendlier method, and that made me passionate about exploring it more.

Later, I pivoted into biopharmaceuticals because I felt that with microbes, one could do even more amazing things. I was committed to the opportunity to make a difference to healthcare in India and abroad. I wanted to reach out to people who didn't have access to these products.

I want young people to know that it is not just about people inspiring you, problems can also inspire you. I am sure some people will inspire you from time to time. But, my driving sense of purpose has been problems. Get inspired by problems that you want to solve for your country and for the world! I believe that sometimes ignorance and not knowledge can actually lead to innovation.

VM: Would you call yourself a goal-driven person?

KM: I am purpose-driven for sure and, obviously, purpose has goals. I was driven by the goal that I wanted to put India on the world map of biotechnology. I felt very proud when India started to get noticed. I also wanted to put Biocon on the map of the world as it relates to diabetes, cancer and autoimmune diseases and, slowly, we are getting there. Such missions drive me!

If you are doing a nine-to-five job without a purpose, it will remain just a job. But, if you add a purpose to the same job, you will not only enjoy it, you will go far beyond the rest. That sense of purpose is what makes ordinary people do extraordinary things!

VM: What, according to you, are leadership skills that are critical for success?

KM: I am a believer of the old adage, 'Lead by example'; don't say one thing and do another. For example, if I say that integrity and accountability are values dear to me, I have to demonstrate them too. A leader has to be fair and not show a bias to certain people. I also believe in the leader being accessible to all people; I leave my door wide open. Anyone with a problem can walk in.

My leadership style is to encourage problem solving. I don't tell people what to do. I tell them to solve the problem. That gives them a purpose and also builds their competence.

I talk straight, I call out wins and failures clearly. I am forthright and I speak my mind. I favour this leadership style and it has worked for me.

VM: Any message to young people on why they should focus on developing leadership skills to do well in their life and career?

KM: First and foremost, I think young people need to be both ambitious and inspired.

Leadership is about decision-making abilities, critical thinking, leading in crisis, empowering yourself and others—everyone should build these abilities.

Leadership is not about 'I–me–myself'. It's about how you can get a team to collaborate and solve problems. It's about getting acceptance from your team.

At the same time, it's not about compromising your own critical thinking. Listen actively, hear everyone out and then take a carefully considered decision. It's a skill to be developed.

When Biocon was in its early phases, I remember having spirited discussions with my team. Visitors to my office would walk in to see me having a massive argument with one of my team members. They'd think that the guy would be fired for speaking his mind. But they'd be surprised to see our conversation ending cordially! That has been my enduring belief: listen well, encourage dissent, be fair, without the assumption that 'I am always right'.

This is particularly true for start-up companies, where leadership can emerge in any role. If you can influence, drive a brainstorming around a suggestion, take people along and be dependable in getting results, you are a leader in that team!

VM: Is there any book you would recommend for young people?

KM: R. Gopalakrishnan wrote a series of books on leaders. He picked success factors astutely. In my case, he picked all the inflection points in my journey that

I used to build the DNA of leadership. That book is *How Kiran Mazumdar-Shaw 'Fermented' Biocon*. Quite interestingly captured! It talks about my strong conviction on everyone being their own self and not imitating others.

So, do read books, take inspiration, but try to be different. Challenge yourself to develop a more differentiated model for yourself!

VM: What would your message to young women be?

KM: Women have latent qualities that they need to discover. I realized that I was ambitious and career-oriented even at a young age.

The family plays an important role; my parents believed in their children. They did not differentiate between me and my two brothers. They invested in each one of us. So, your family needs to invest in you, build your confidence and make you feel that you can succeed as much as your brother can.

We had a lot of mutual awe between the siblings. While I admired my brother's IIT entry and his brilliance in math and computer science, he was equally in admiration of my achievements in the area of biological sciences and my choice to study brewing.

Women should demand the opportunities they need. Push yourself a lot more.

VM: How can women develop more self-belief?

KM: Learn from women who have notched up achievements at diverse levels. I am on the Infosys board as an independent director, and when we are looking for board members, I can tell you there are some excellent women leaders around the world.

Women need to know that this tribe of women leaders has grown exponentially. When looking for examples to seek inspiration from, don't just look at the iconic examples, look at levels just above you! Look at women you can relate to, the smart young women around you who are doing some amazing stuff.

Don't get daunted by the highly successful women out there. Know that the opportunities that you have access to are much more than what we had in our times. So, think big and make the most of the potential and opportunities you have.

Dr Devi Shetty on Role Models, Goals and the Future of Medicine

Dr Devi Prasad Shetty, a cardiac surgeon, is the founder, chairman and executive director of Narayana Health, a hospital chain that revolutionized health and cardiac care. He also initiated the concept of the 'micro health insurance scheme' in Karnataka, which was the source of the government's Yeshasvini scheme, a micro health insurance scheme for rural farmers.

He is the recipient of a number of awards and honours, most noteworthy being the Padma Shri and Padma Bhushan in 2003 and 2012 respectively, conferred by the Government of India, and the Rajyotsava Award conferred by the Government of Karnataka in 2002. He is a professor at Rajiv Gandhi University of Medical Sciences, Bengaluru, India and the University of Minnesota Medical School, USA.

He also received the Outstanding Social Entrepreneurship Award conferred by the Confederation of Indian Industry in 2005, the President's Award by the American College of Cardiology in 2011 and the *Economic Times* Entrepreneur of the Year Award in 2012. Further, he received the Indian of the Year Award in 2012 by CNN–IBN and the Lifetime Achievement Award by the Federation of Indian Chambers of Commerce and Industry. In addition, he received a commendation for driving affordable quality healthcare for all in 2010 at the Healthcare Awards Programme presented by ICICI Lombard and CNBC-TV18 and was the winner of the Business Process Award at *The Economist* Innovation Awards 2011.

Brimming with the love of life, the ever-smiling doctor comes through like a poet with a deeply sensitive view on life and success in this interview.

VM: Dr Shetty, as a child and while growing up, who were the people who inspired you?

DS: I think my first role model was my father, a hero whom I watched every day. How he, despite not being very educated and with humble beginnings, managed six or seven hotels single-handedly.

With Indian Independence fresh in our minds, Chandrashekhar Azad and Subhash Chandra Bose inspired me to do something for my country.

When I was in the fifth standard, my teacher shared the news with us about a breakthrough heart transplant having been done in South Africa. I was immensely inspired by this doctor and decided to become a heart surgeon.

I was the eighth of nine children in my family, and one of the consequences of that was that my parents had aged by the time I was in my teens. My father was diabetic and hospital trips became very frequent. In that phase, all the doctors I encountered became heroes I looked up to.

Then, my oldest brother became a doctor and he became a role model to me.

Let me share a thought on role models. Immediately after Tenzing Norgay and Edmund Hillary scaled Mount Everest, there was a flood of people replicating their feat in a very short time! Mount Everest hadn't changed. People hadn't suddenly become stronger. Those things had remained the same. It is just that someone had proven that it was doable. That had become a huge inspiration. That's the power of role models.

VM: Tell me about the goals you set. Were you always a goal-driven person?

DS: The heroes I had while growing up must surely have given me goals and inspiration somewhere deep inside. But I always had a goal, it was that I wanted to touch millions of people and change their lives positively. My paths would have changed, sometimes significantly altered, but the goal has remained the same.

Let me share a story that comes to my mind when I am asked this question. Let's say we are in a stormy sea alone in a boat, trying desperately to direct it to the shore using the rudder. We are clinging to that lever, trying to guide the boat in adverse conditions. Somehow, and after a big struggle, we manage to reach the shore. We are so relieved and also proud of our steering skills. But we must realize that only a small rudder was in our hand!

So, acknowledging the role of the Almighty in life is important.

VM: What are three critical success factors that made you who you are today?

DS: The first and foremost is compassion. If you want to be a successful doctor you need to have a strong sense of compassion. As a young doctor, while working in rural areas, I regularly dealt with patients who were in a bad shape. So much so that some doctors did not even want to stand close to them, let alone touch them. They were unhygienic, had oozing ulcers and maggots crawling in their wounds. But honestly, I didn't feel even a bit of revulsion. I was just happy being of help to them.

The second one is skill. I wasn't one of those outstanding students in college, but one thing about me is that I love working with my fingers! As a kid, I would dismantle and assemble every machine that was available! And now, my fingers have made me into a skilled surgeon.

Third, I have worked many, many times harder than most of my colleagues. While others might work three to four days a week, I would be operating sixteen to eighteen hours a day, seven days a week. Well, the practice and hard work, quite naturally, made me better.

Finally, I love what I do.

VM: What are your views on innovation?

DS: We, as humans, tend to think that the world will remain the same and that the future is an extension of the past. This is quite far from the truth!

When we keep innovating, we keep making the world a better place to live in.

If you want to innovate and create, no one can stop you. The beauty of the universe is that everything that we need for the welfare of the human being has already been created by nature; we have to just keep on unpeeling it and exploring its potential.

When my daughter was five or six years old, she was very good at doing jigsaw puzzles. The entire house would be littered with puzzle pieces when I would come home. Once, seeing her straining herself over a complicated puzzle, I told her to leave it. She replied, 'But Daddy, the pieces are right here!' That is the summary: all the answers are out there; we only need to have the determination to keep looking for them.

VM: What does excellence mean to you?

DS: Whenever we finish operating on the heart, I always tell my colleagues that if it looks beautiful, it works! If there is symmetry, if all the sutures look neat and uniform, it means the surgery has worked. I ask, 'Does the heart look happy?' That is excellence for me! It is not just about completing a job, it's about completing it beautifully. One can operate on the heart and leave it looking like a dog's dinner and call it a success because the patient has made it. Not me.

That is why I have huge respect for Apple products; they are well made, embody beauty, and take into consideration what the consumer feels and values.

Look at your output and ask yourself if it is beautiful and making you happy. That is the test of excellence!

VM: What are your thoughts on work–life balance?

DS: Well, if you've chosen medicine as a profession, I don't think there is going to be much of a work–life balance. I am passionate about my work, I enjoy my work and can work for eighteen hours a day and still keep smiling. In fact, sometimes, operations go on till 11 p.m. When I think of work–life balance, I am reminded of that soldier at Siachen Glacier. Does he have any of it?

While I may not have as much time for the family as people in other professions do, I deeply value the family time I get. I play with my grandchildren, I sit and talk with my family members. I really enjoy it. But, not having a lot of time for family does not mean that I don't value them. They are my entire lifeline.

I believe that people who want to make a difference in the world should manage their work–life balance differently.

VM: What changes do you foresee in the future that students of medicine should know about?

DS: Technology in medicine will take over. I believe that the largest healthcare provider is going to be a software and hardware with beds attached to it. Decisions on patient care will be made by smart algorithms that will be smarter than human doctors. In the future, it will become legally mandatory for doctors to get a second opinion from the algorithm before starting treatment. Of course, the doctor can override that, but it will become a norm.

There won't be paper and pen any more. All those nurses in the intensive care unit jotting down details will be assisted by machines that will have real-time electronic medical records. Not only records, these machines will build intelligence to anticipate and predict events. For example, a patient has certain bodily changes about six hours before they have a cardiac arrest: the blood gases change, acidosis happens, urine output goes down and so on. The machine can note all this and predict the cardiac arrest, giving precious time to doctors to manage the challenge.

To sum up, if you have the entire day to look at a patient, the human mind is definitely smarter, but if you are in a crunch situation and cannot spend that much time with the patient, the machine is smarter.

The future will be based on the interaction between man/woman and machine.

Medical students should be prepared to be technologically savvy and to learn new ways of offering medical care.

John Chambers on Passion, Mentoring and Leadership

John Chambers served as CEO, chairman and executive chairman of Cisco Systems. During his twenty-five-plus years at Cisco, he helped grow the company from $70 million when he joined in 1991 to $1.2 billion when he became CEO in 1995, to $47 billion when he stepped down as CEO in 2015.

Chambers was awarded the Padma Bhushan by the Government of India in 2019 for his contributions to trade and the tech industry in India. He has received numerous awards for his leadership in business as well, including being named the number two among the Best-Performing CEOs in the World in 2015 by *Harvard Business Review*, one of *Barron's* World's Best CEOs, and one of *Time* magazine's 100 Most Influential People. He also received the Edison Achievement Award for Innovation and was awarded the Outstanding Civil Service Medal by the US Army, as well as France's National Defence Gold Medal, the only foreign business leader to ever receive the award in its thirty-nine-year history.

Today, he is focused on his role as the founder and CEO of JC2 Ventures. Chambers is helping disruptive start-ups from around the world build and scale, while also promoting the broader development of start-up nations and a start-up world.

I have spent some wonderful times with John during my tenure at Cisco. On my last visit to his home, he presented me with a signed copy of his book *Connecting the Dots*, which I highly recommend.

VM: What, according to you, are the top three factors that led to your success?

JC: Both of my parents were doctors. My mom was a psychiatrist, and Dad was an OB-GYN who delivered around 6000 babies, including all four of Senator Jay Rockefeller's kids. My mom taught me how to build emotional connections and Dad taught me how to think and plan. My parents and my extended family taught me invaluable life lessons about dreaming big, never giving up, staying calm during crises and so much more.

The second factor was a keen understanding of the market and the ability to get market transitions right, rather than competing against my competitors.

Third, I kept it simple. I asked, 'What does the customer want?' and then worked on supplying it. I have no love of technology for technology's sake—my main focus is solutions for customers.

'John Chambers is the most customer-focused human being you will ever meet.'
                                        —Venture capitalist John Doerr

VM: Have you been goal-driven since you were young?

JC: When I would swim laps or catch fish as a kid, and now as I help build successful start-up teams, I have always had fun competing. I was absolutely goal-driven when I was young and continue to be to this day. I set high goals for Cisco to reach from $1 billion to $47 billion during my tenure as CEO. I also worked as hard as I could to meet my goal of never missing my morning jog, family priorities or fishing expeditions.

VM: What role has passion played for you?

JC: I'm passionate about everything I do—and even now I am passionate in my new chapter as a venture capitalist. I wake up every morning excited to start my day—I've never had so much fun! I love giving back and motivating others to achieve goals that they never thought were possible. When I look back on my career, I think that passion played off during a number of difficult times as well. To me, passion was key in ensuring that Cisco had a very low turnover rate. As you know, Vivek, most people stayed on with us for a long time. I believe in building a family at the workplace and that is driven by passion.

VM: What are your thoughts on excellence, which is becoming the best version of yourself?

JC: I believe in 'Do it right and do it to the fullest'. I time myself while running and try to beat my time every time. I wanted to change the world through job creation and that is what I am trying to do, as best as I can. Thinking about excellence, I guess, to me, it is more about excellence as a team. Now, I try to achieve that by helping my start-ups set goals and mentor them to stretch and achieve those goals, to help build a more digital, sustainable future.

VM: In addition to professional goals, which other goals are important to you?

JC: Definitely, one goal has been giving back to society, helping build houses or feeding the needy. Another one is family. Let me do some quick math here: I think we've got eighteen married couples in a family of four generations and never a divorce; that is not just luck. I strongly believe that things don't just work out, you have to step up to it. I'm also a believer in play hard, work hard!

VM: What is the role of mentors in your journey?

JC: We all need mentors. Instead of making your own mistakes, you can learn from others'—and the good news is, it's a lot less painful!

I think there were many people who influenced me and played the role of mentor in my journey, starting with my parents. I am very fortunate to have had amazing parents. My mom broke gender barriers in many ways, to become a doctor, athlete, ballroom dancer, lifeguard, ping-pong champion.

Growing up being dyslexic wasn't easy. When I was in second grade, my teachers were pretty concerned that I wouldn't graduate. Mrs Anderson, my third-grade tutor, helped me overcome my stumbling blocks. She taught me to read reasonably well and then how to take it to the next level and use my disability as an advantage. I definitely would not have been able to get degrees in business and law without her.

I have also had the fortune to have many amazing advisers over the years, from Henry Kissinger to Shimon Peres to Bill Clinton and George Bush. Today I am enjoying the give and take I have with French President Emmanuel Macron and Prime Minister Narendra Modi, who is one of the top leaders in the world today.

VM: What are the expectations of leaders in current times?

JC: The CEO has a few key responsibilities: identify the strategy and vision, develop the management team, create the culture and communicate on all of the above. In addition to really understanding their industry/field/ philosophy, leaders need to have the ability to see what changes are occurring and outline a strategy that helps their company disrupt itself over and over again. Leaders need to take risks and move fast. It is better to stumble first than arrive last. First movers face the biggest risks but get more attention, opportunity and leeway to make mistakes.

VM: What kind of culture do you recommend that start-ups build right from the start?

JC: You can never have a great company without a great culture. Look at Cisco or Oracle or Microsoft or Walmart; they all have strong cultures.

As you (as a business) start to grow, you get to know what culture works for you. Whether it's a customer–first or a family approach to the business, you will want to be consistent in what you say and what you do. It might sound basic but if you just do the right thing, your culture will guide almost every decision you make.

VM: How important are relationships to you, and what would you do if they came in conflict with your professional goals?

JC: I build relationships and friendships for life. You may remember that, during my time at Cisco, I was very connected with the employee population, in addition to the management team. There were countless times I remember sitting on the phone late at night with employees, helping them come up with an action plan to help give a sick relative their best fighting chance.

More important than both relationships and professional goals are my ethics. I have taken a tough stand when those are being challenged. I have always made my family the centrepiece of decisions.

We were taught values and lessons throughout generations, guiding us to do the right thing on the most basic issues. Treat others as well as you would treat yourself.

I bet my job at Cisco two times, when the board of directors was asking something of me that I wasn't comfortable with. I told my wife about it and, jointly, we decided to stick to our principles. Both issues were a decade apart, and I kept my job both times. So, while professional goals are important, one needs to back up the commitments one makes to one's value system and family also! Relationships and trust need to be protected because those are the cornerstones of business today. The currency of our world is your track record, your relationships and your trust.

VM: What would be your advice to youth?

JC: Be your own person, don't copy someone else. Be comfortable being who you are. Have the courage to dream. Set goals, accomplish them! Don't compromise your values, do the right thing. Picture the outcome in your mind, and then go for it. Be disruptive, show courage and don't panic.

I also say—and this might surprise your readers—you can never be too prepared for a meeting, presentation, interview, or even business dinner. The best spontaneous conversations or discussions are the ones that are well-rehearsed in advance.

'Chambers doesn't attend meetings blind. He has a playbook—and an objective. Before meeting with anyone, Chambers makes sure he's well informed. He has an assistant or publicist create a 1-inch-thick binder—a playbook—for the day's meetings, presentations, sales calls or press interviews. It contains the bios of every person he's scheduled to meet, data on what his company is doing for that person or community, background clips, a summary of objectives for every meeting, and speaking notes for presentations.'

—John Chambers' Chief of Staff

Rahul Dravid on Excellence

Rahul Dravid is one of the finest batsmen India and the world has ever produced, earning himself nicknames like 'The Wall' and 'Mr Dependable'. In his one-day-international career, he amassed more than 10,000 runs and, in 164 tests, he accumulated more than 13,000 runs. He scored 36 hundreds and 63 fifties in his Test career. He is also the second-highest run-getter for India in test matches. He's the only batsman to have scored a century in *every* test-playing nation. He has been honoured with the Arjuna Award, Padma Shri and Padma Bhushan for his achievements.

> *'I have never seen a more dedicated cricketer than Rahul in the nets. He was able to simulate a game situation, not just by going through the motions but by making every ball count. It was like he didn't want to get out even in the nets. In a situation when we had three or four bowlers going at him, he wanted to compete. He was always testing himself . . .'*
> —John Wright, coach of the Indian team

Rahul Dravid must have been told a million times, if not more, that his equanimity and his commitment to calm toughness and perseverance have left us cricket-lovers awestruck. Still, I noticed the shy smile creeping up his face when I said it. In this interview, I asked this magician about his magic wand. He said, matter-offactly, that there is no such wand: just a set of skills and passionate perseverance, and a relentless drive towards excellence.

Rahul is a family friend and my entire family adores him. Our discussions on excellence and life's goals have always been extremely fulfilling and insightful. Even though I have met him countless times, every time I meet him, he elevates me with the sheer positivity of his energy.

VM: What does excellence mean to you?

RD: To me, excellence is the constant effort to get the best out of myself. To begin with, one has to recognize the skills one possesses for the chosen pursuit and then figure out if a huge reserve of passion accompanies it. For me, I was fortunate to have a skill set suited for the game of cricket. I had tremendous passion, even as a child, to pursue the game. Though it started out as a hobby, it became the largest part of my life pretty quickly.

Excellence is a continuous journey. There are no rest stops. You have to keep evaluating your progress and improving. You need not compare yourself with others all the time, but review yourself against your chosen goals. Hence, set your goals in clear and unambiguous language.

Excellence is also about being introspective. You need to look deep within—without wearing blinders or coloured glasses. You have to be brutal about where you are lacking and need to improve.

VM: What was the most important part of your journey towards excellence?

RD: There were many high and low points in the journey, but what mattered to me most was that, at the end of it, I could walk out of the stadium with my head held high and without any regrets. Everyone needs to create a process and plan that keeps him or her on the path to excellence.

VM: What's the hardest part in the path to excellence?

RD: I'd say it's the constant perseverance towards seeing challenges as opportunities and the passion to improve. Even when you are at the pinnacle and enjoying a fair amount of success, how you can still be focused on improving further is the key. The pursuit of excellence is not a part-time or some-time investment, it is an all-the-time thing. Commitment, discipline and drive are needed in good measure. And, of course, a deep love and passion for what you do.

VM: Was there a turning point in your journey towards excellence?

RD: Yes, getting dropped from the one-day team in 1998 forced me to introspect, recalibrate and relearn. I was out of the one-day team for a year, during which I spent a massive amount of time developing new skills and adapting my game for the one-day arena. It took a lot, beginning with a deeper awareness of the finer aspects of what I lacked and, subsequently, the hard work to improve. I was able to play ten years of one-day cricket after that and score over 10,000 runs in over 300 one-day matches.

John Wright noted that: 'He never made the same mistake twice. He learnt hugely in one-day cricket—which probably was an area he had to work at a little bit more than others. He had been dropped from the Indian one-day team and then went on to come back and have a very good World Cup [in 2003].'

VM: What is the recipe for excellence?

RD: Apart from what I described earlier, it's also in the little things. All of those little things that come together to shape you. For a sportsperson, it could be the practice, the introspection, the attitude and the diet, to name some. And how one can be honest about these things even when no one is watching. It is in the sacrifices that you make during your pursuit, even in small things such as how much sleep you are getting. Those give you that extra 5 per cent edge over others. I have found that honesty is so important, that is, the kind of honesty one needs with oneself. So, be honest with your own self!

You need clarity of thought—every decision you make comes with its pros and cons—it's important to evaluate and 'own' each decision. Spend time to introspect on what you want in life. It's not always about what you can achieve but also what makes you happy, like you and I have often discussed, Vivek.

VM: How have coaches helped you in your journey towards excellence?

RD: Keki Tarapore was my first coach and a true inspirer. He had great passion and love for cricket. But, as you move ahead in your journey, you play for different team compositions and under different circumstances. So, your coaching needs to change. Having said that, one cannot discount the importance of having different mentors and coaches at different phases of one's career. They are the extra pair of eyes you need to help you learn more about yourself and improve.

VM: What's your advice for a balanced life?

RD: As a sportsman, I was travelling eight to nine months in a year. So, it was far from balanced, but I was aware of it and did the best with whatever family time I had. However, I realigned my goals after retirement and made some difficult choices, let go some lucrative contracts, to make sure I compensated for it. One thing I did throughout was that I did not let my success or failure determine who I was as a person. I stayed 'balanced' for the family. Having a good family and friend environment helps release pressure, it helps one stay sane in tough times. I strongly believe in investing in relationships.

VM: How does one demonstrate excellence in a team situation?

RD: Begin with being excellent as an individual. Cricket is an individual game within a team game. When you give the best version of yourself to the team, it raises the bar for others too. You also need to recognize that in order to be the best version of yourself, you need other people. If I am practising in the nets, I need a bowler, for example. You need to recognize and contribute towards creating healthy relationships.

VM: What is your message to readers on pursuing excellence?

RD: Each one of us needs to realize our potential and become the best version of ourselves to do well in our careers and life. So, it is worth putting in your best effort to pursue excellence.

Prakash Padukone on Family Values and Relationships

In 1962, when a seven-year-old started playing badminton with his father, who knew he'd go on to dominate the national badminton scene for almost a decade (1971–80) and put India *on the sport's international map?*

Prakash Padukone won the national championship in 1971 at age sixteen followed by nine national titles in a row. In 1978, he won the singles badminton gold medal at the Commonwealth Games. The following year, he won both the Danish Open and the Swedish Open. His greatest accomplishment came in 1980 when he became the first Indian to win the All-England Championships, the world's most prestigious annual badminton competition.

He was honoured with the Arjuna Award and Padma Shri for his sporting achievements. The wristy style of this artist was always heavy on aggression of other players, and his shy, humble demeanour belies the strength of a great human being who has notched up many wins while keeping family values intact. He is the proud father of Deepika (actor) and Anisha (golfer), and he lives in Bangalore with his wife, Ujjala.

Having known the Padukone family for several years, I have always appreciated Prakash's focus on family relationships and values. I have been struck by his humility and down-to-earth attitude in spite of his godlike achievements.

VM: Who was the first person from your family who inspired you?

PP: 'You have to take life as it comes,' my father once said. He showed me how one needs to stay positive and focused. After work, he would take me to play in a club which was basically a marriage hall, since a proper badminton court wasn't that easily accessible. He taught me how to focus on what I have, work hard and enjoy the process, more than getting anxious about the outcome. I learnt to 'refuse to complain', that is, work with whatever resources I had and make the most of those. That, I'd say, was the bedrock for everything I achieved.

VM: How significant are family values for you?

PP: Family values are very important to me. My wife, Ujjala, and I have tried to teach the right values to our daughters, Deepika and Anisha, right from their childhood. We have told them that there is no substitute for perseverance, hard work, determination and passion for what you choose to do. If you love what you do, nothing else matters. We celebrate each other. For instance, I am fine being introduced as Deepika's father just as she is equally proud of being introduced as Prakash's daughter.

Just as my father let me spread my wings and choose whichever career I wanted, I have let my daughters also follow their passion. I feel that parents have to recognize the child's passion and encourage that regardless of whatever beliefs they personally hold.

Being disciplined and being a good human being have been strong values for all four of us. We have always given high importance to letting each other express ourselves openly and being authentic. As I always say, in the end, when your career is behind you, what remains with you and for you is family, and the friends that you have made who will stand by you. Hence, we need to live the kind of life that will allow us to be true to our own conscience.

VM: How have you nurtured close relationships in your family?

PP: We are a close-knit family tied with strong relationships. We spent as much quality time with my daughters as possible, especially when they were young. We would make it a point to have dinner together at the dining table to the extent possible. Now, whenever we meet, we talk transparently about our values, passions and dreams. We give each other advice and listen to each other.

We are a rooted family. My daughters sleep on the floor if we have house guests. They make their own beds and help clean up after dinner even now, when they are visiting.

VM: Could you share a fond ritual (similar to the American Thanksgiving) that the Padukone family observes to periodically renew relationship ties?

PP: When the kids were young, we would religiously go on two vacations, summer and winter. Even now we have fond memories of those trips.

VM. How have you both instilled family values in your family?

PP: We give a lot of importance to relationships, honesty, and respect for parents and elders. Material success is important but not fundamental to happiness and peace of mind. We recognize the value of peace of mind and good health. We trust in the rejuvenating power of prayers and offering prayers is a long-standing tradition in our family.

We have been strict where we had to be and lenient at times depending on the situation. More than that, we have tried to set an example to our daughters by what we did (our actions) more than what we said (our words). Ujjala and I try to be good role models and live by the family values we care about. Vivek, like you say, 'Be what you want your children to be.'

In badminton, it's always one point at a time. Similarly, in life, it's one step at a time. We have encouraged both our children to build their careers one step at a time, with utmost perseverance.

VM: What are your suggestions to the younger generation on developing family relationships?

PP: Spend quality time together. Try to have at least one meal a day together at the dining table without TV and cell phones, discussing things that happened during the day. Try to go on family vacations at least once every six months; invest deeply in your family.

I strongly believe that it is important to try to be the best in whatever you do, regardless of money. Always focus on what you want to become as an individual, and empower yourself to reach your goals without distractions and without compromising your values.

Vinita Bali on Leadership and Thinking Outside the Box

Vinita Bali is a global business leader with extensive experience in successfully leading large multinational corporations in senior business and marketing roles. Vinita was most recently chief executive officer and managing director of Britannia Industries Ltd. Prior to Britannia, Vinita spent nearly a decade with Coca-Cola in several roles, including vice president and head, corporate strategy, based in the US; president, Andean Division, based in Chile; and worldwide marketing director, based in the US. Prior to that, she spent fourteen years with Cadbury, serving in senior marketing roles across a number of geographies, including South Africa, Nigeria, India and the UK.

She has been awarded Businesswoman of the Year at the *Economic Times* Awards. Vinita currently serves on the board of directors of Cognizant, Bunge Ltd, Syngene International Ltd and CRISIL Ltd. She holds a bachelor's degree in economics from the University of Delhi, India, and an MBA degree from Jamnalal Bajaj Institute of Management Studies, Mumbai, India.

Vinita is a dear friend of the family; we all look up to her and enjoy our enriching interactions whenever we meet.

VM: What, according to you, are the top three factors that led to your success?

VB: I have a nice short form for it: ACE.

A—Attitude: We can't control our environment of success but can control how we deal with it. Do we see the glass as half full or half empty?

C—Curiosity: Even in school, I was a curious child. I was there in the top five academically but, more importantly, I took a great deal of interest in sports, theatre, elocution, Indian classical art, dancing. I was always surrounded by a lot of stimuli that moulded and shaped my curiosity.

E—Striving for Excellence: It's just plain and simple hard work that is needed! As Salvador Dali said, 'Have no fear of perfection—you'll never reach it!' I never aim for perfection. I don't even like the word *perfection*. But I am never satisfied with mediocrity or a *chalta hai* attitude.

VM: Are you a goal-driven person?

VB: I never set goals in terms of wanting to become a CEO or head of marketing. I am more of an organic person. However, one goal that has been a constant since my student days, more of a question is, 'Am I enjoying what I am doing?' and 'Am I doing it well enough?'

To elaborate, I love to travel; hence, I wanted to join the foreign services. I figured that an Indian foreign service job would take me all over the globe. But when I got into JBIMS, Mumbai, a cousin told me that I could always write the IFS exams after doing an MBA. Post that, I got a job with Voltas. And that was the end of my foreign service dreams.

My goal was to go after what brings me joy. As Maya Angelou said, 'Success is liking yourself, liking what you do, and liking how you do it.' So, you can say that I am driven by excellence, becoming the best version of myself, like you always say, Vivek.

VM: Any example of thinking out of the box?

VB: I feel that part of leadership is about having your antennae up all the time, absorbing all the signals and figuring out what role you can play. So, when I was at Britannia, which was a supplier to the World Food Programme of the United Nations, one of our interesting products was the calorie-dense biscuits that were supplied to areas ravaged by natural disasters or war. At the same time, I read an article on the health and nutrition status in India, and then I got acquainted with a Swiss foundation in Geneva, which I ended up chairing later, called the Global Alliance for Improved Nutrition. They talked about using micronutrient-based fortification to address 'hidden hunger', which is about someone getting enough calories but not the vitamins and minerals that are needed. That led to an incredible insight in my entire group and myself at Britannia. Why not take the 'biscuit' that is a pervasive food item and use it as a carrier of micronutrients—what a vast difference it could make! That led us to partner with the Nandi Foundation and Akshaya Patra to supply iron-fortified biscuits. Driving such a structural, systemic innovation was amazing.

VM: What does leadership mean to you?

VB: Leadership is a verb: it isn't a title or a position, it's behaviour—what I do and how I do it. Therefore, even as a management trainee, you can display leadership.

Effective leadership is about being self-aware to the highest degree possible. It's also about being empathetic, that is, having harmonious relations with people and even the environment, including the tree outside your window.

Leadership is also about transformation. Am I making this place better than what it was in a manner that is inclusive and that will be sustainable and enduring? It's about caring. It's about the ability to envision what you want to create. Paint a vivid picture. Once you have a clear end state, you will get there. You might take some detours, but you will reach it!

Leadership is about operating with integrity, being authentic and displaying good judgement and character under duress or pressure. The choices that you make become very relevant when you have a choice. Not just financial, there is intellectual integrity as well.

The entry point in an organization is through skills and education. But people who separate themselves from the rest on account of their leadership skills move forward.

VM: How did you develop your leadership skills?

VB: Initially, it was a conscious process. At the Convent of Jesus and Mary, I was captain of my class and later, head girl of the school. In Lady Sriram College, I was vice president and then president of the student union.

When you are in such roles, you are representing people and need to get things done for them. These roles helped me expand my horizon. It was no longer only about me. It had become me *plus* all other people. It was a self-reinforcing loop that gave me tremendous confidence.

I need to give a lot of credit to my parents for keeping the atmosphere at home liberal. We children could voice opposing points of view without fear.

I never think that something is not possible. My adrenaline goes when there is a problem—I want to solve issues even if I don't have the answers. I am excited about what I can do and what others can do.

VM: What has been the role of role models or mentors in your life?

VB: I had many role models. Often, not the person per se, but the behaviour he or she exhibited. I have a beautiful memory of an aunt in Delhi who had moved to India post Partition and wasn't that well-off, socio-economically. But she was dearly loved by everybody. I was a little child, but I was soon to find out why.

We used to have milk booths in Delhi from where milk arrived at our doorstep in bottles. The empty bottles had to be returned to the booth. My aunt would fill those returnable bottles with cold water for the people manning those booths. In the terribly hot summers, it was a boon to the staff crammed in the booths. Slowly, this practice caught on and became a trend. I really admired her for this empathetic behaviour and simple way to give back.

Another impactful memory is from the School of Indian Classical Music Dance that was next to my house. Several top-notch artistes would perform there, for instance, Pt Ravi Shankar, Ali Akbar Khan, Hirabai Barodekar, Girija Devi, Manilal Nag and so many others. Pt Nikhil Banerjee, the top sitar player in those days, used to stay there when in town. He would get up at 5 a.m. to do his *riyaz*. We woke up to the sounds of his sitar. What a role model of dedication to hone his skills, day after day. No complacency!

Books also have introduced me to wonderful role models. For instance, Madame Curie and her intense curiosity to understand the principles of chemistry.

VM: What is your message for the youth of India?

VB: Look at your life as the opportunity to change things not just for yourself but also your family, society, planet. Whatever your sphere of influence. Don't be afraid to lead or follow, as long as you are driving positive change. You don't have to have the answers, but be smart to know where to look for answers. Don't wait for someone to tell you to do something. Just look at the world—what is the kind of world that you want to inhabit and how will you contribute to building it?

VM: Is there a book that you'd like to recommend?

VB: There are several, but I absolutely love these two biographies:

- Marie Curie's biography
- Maria Callas's biography

Vani Kola on Entrepreneurship

Vani Kola is the founder and managing director of Kalaari Capital, one of India's leading early-stage venture capital firms. She is a proponent of India's digital opportunity to create next-gen large-scale companies, which will scale globally.

Having built two successful companies in Silicon Valley, Vani's investment philosophy is derived from her entrepreneurial experiences. Vani has led more than thirty investments at Kalaari in e-commerce, gaming, digital content, healthcare and more. Some of her successes include Dream11, Myntra, Curefit and Snapdeal. She currently serves on the board of several companies that are redefining the landscape of Indian business.

Over the last decade, Vani has become an influential voice in the country's vibrant start-up ecosystem. She has been profiled in numerous books and has been identified as one of *Fortune India*'s Most Powerful Women in Business.

I admire Vani for her achievements, and she's quite the poster girl for 'been there, done that'. She is a family friend and we have deep admiration for each other's families.

VM: What, according to you, are the top three factors that led to your success?

VK: In my life, there have been so many people who have knowingly or unknowingly contributed to my success. I cannot attribute it just to my hard work or focus. I want to take out the word *me*. Our efforts are not enough alone.

Firstly, my parents had a relentless commitment to their children's education. I cannot imagine that in different family circumstances, I would have had the fundamentals to achieve success.

Secondly, very serendipitously, I ended up in Silicon Valley. The environment there was a huge influence. That put me in the direction of entrepreneurship and a lifelong quest for learning.

Thirdly, the 'early believers' and mentors in my life. You have to find these early believers because they see something intangible in you. Not your pedigree or bank balance. These are folks who see something in you and encourage you. They are there to show you a better mirror than you can see yourself.

For example, even when I had notched up some level of success and was coming back to India, there were several naysayers, but I had some early believers who said, 'That's interesting' or 'I can see why you will definitely succeed'. I am sure you also faced the same challenges, Vivek, when you decided to come back to India.

In addition, if I were to pick specifics, I'd say firstly, the deep analytical training I received through math and engineering, and later, computer science, created an embedded ability to problem-solve. That was a great hard skill to have. A second specific skill would be the ability to take risks and not be afraid to fail. I could see a future worth pursuing even if there was a chance that it wouldn't work. Risk-taking doesn't mean that you jump from a plane without a parachute. You take *calculated risks*. A third skill was to keep a long-term focus in every decision I made. There were always short-term compromises and setbacks but I never let go of the long-term goal.

VM: Were you always goal-driven? If not, when did you start setting goals for yourself?

VK: I think I always had overall goals—like 'Do well in math' or 'Do engineering' or 'Keep learning'. At that point, I did not have outcome goals, such as 'I want to be a CEO'.

I went hiking in Bhutan, that's something I had always wanted to do. We were targeting some tough heights. I hadn't trained much. The guide made an observation: 'You must be doing yoga.' He explained that the only way I was able to scale the peaks was because I took deep breaths. The lesson is that 'walking each step' can be a goal as much as 'scaling the peak'. I had broken the goal into twenty steps at a time.

Another goal I have always had is to have a strong, rooted family. Quite early on, this was a goal I had placed in my 'important bucket'. Once you have identified an important goal, everything else has to be worked out in its context. Right now, my children ask me if I will visit them, but my parents are old and I can't leave them alone here. So, I tell my children that they can come and visit but I can't since I cannot leave my parents for a month. Goals, hence, are also about a principle that provides a compass.

VM: What made you successful as an entrepreneur? What were some rewards and costs?

VK: I evaluated myself a lot. I figured that I had multiple dimensions to my personality and capability in addition to being an engineer and I thought I could utilize those—so entrepreneurship to me was a test to myself. My journey was one of self-discovery and pushing myself to my limit.

The reward of this journey is one of deep self-fulfilment, and the feeling one gets when pushed to one's limits to learn. The dopamine reward is the best one.

The costs of the journey are about making tough prioritizing calls. For example, not spending time with friends. I didn't compromise on family—we went to social events and parties where we could take the kids. Well, 'me' time was often compromised, but never family!

VM: What are the top five skills for aspiring entrepreneurs?

VK: The first one is core conviction: What are you doing and why are you doing it? You have to keep asking this question. You need lots of conviction, because ninety-nine people out of 100 will discourage you.

The second one is the ability to listen. Listen *actively*. If you have conviction but not the ability to listen, it's a problem. You have to listen, filter and take feedback.

The third is grit. It's that voice that says, 'Just do it'. Remember, nothing comes free and it's a really bumpy ride.

The fourth is 'width', that is, how big is your purpose. Your leadership will be limited or expanded by your capacity to increase your purpose, how inclusive you are. One could be to build a large organization and make money. Nothing wrong with that. But for larger success, your purpose needs to be broader.

The fifth one is continuous learning. Don't think, 'I am the boss, hence I should have all the answers.' Have the humility to reach out to people who may know something in any directly or indirectly related field, and have the appetite to learn.

VM: Why should our Indian youth focus on entrepreneurship?

VK: Firstly, we are lucky to be in an era where entrepreneurship is possible, valued and needed. Particularly in India, there is a huge amount of opportunity.

Secondly, we have very skilled youth with the right skills.

Thirdly, there isn't any huge downside. Think of how much employment you can generate and with that, contribute to the economic development of our country!

VM: What has been the role of role models and mentors in your life?

VK: For role models, I love reading biographies. I read voraciously about people from many walks of life. I try to delve into what that person was thinking and how I can learn from it.

Mentors are close to you and have your situation's context. I have had many mentors. When I first started out, the people at TiE, The Indus Entrepreneur, were willing to give me time and help me grow. Sometimes, they met me every week. Currently, I have two go-to people to help me bounce off all thoughts.

Choose mentors whom you trust. They must have some context and you should permit them to say anything, totally candidly.

Ramesh and Swati Ramanathan on Giving Back to Society

Ramesh Ramanathan is a social entrepreneur and works on urban issues in India. He is co-founder of the Janaagraha Centre for Citizenship and Democracy, a non-profit organization focused on transforming the quality of life in urban India. He works closely with central and many state governments on urban issues as an adviser. He has contributed as the national technical adviser, Government of India for the Jawaharlal Nehru National Urban Renewal Mission, the country's flagship urban mission.

Prior to his social initiatives, Ramesh held leadership positions with Citibank in New York and London, in the bank's capital markets business. Ramesh has an MS in physics from BITS Pilani, an MBA from Yale University and a CFA from AIMR. In 2007, he was chosen as a Young Global Leader by the World Economic Forum.

Swati Ramanathan, co-founder of Janaagraha, leads its innovation in the use of social media and mobile and Internet technology for civic participation. She has received international awards and recognition for ipaidabribe.com, an online platform for reducing retail corruption, and for ichangemycity.com on hyperlocal citizen participation.

In 2007, Swati was named Young Asian Leader by the Asia Society. In 2008, she was honoured by the

Government of Rajasthan with the Rajyotsava Puraskar for her work on the Jaipur 2025 master plan. In 2013, Swati was honoured by the National Democratic Institute in Washington DC, with the Democracy and Civic Innovator Award. In 2013, she and Ramesh were honoured with the Social Entrepreneurs of the Year Award by *Forbes India*. Swati holds a BS from India, and an MS from Pratt Institute, New York.

This outstanding couple left their glittering careers abroad, and returned to India with stars in their eyes and a vision to give back to their homeland. In 2001, Bangalore sported billboards that said: 'Here are a few fools like Nandan Nilekani, Vishnuvardhan, Dr Devi Shetty and Syed Kirmani who think they can change Bangalore. If you are also a fool, then call us.' Around 5000 volunteers showed up. Soon, Janaagraha was born. Janaagraha envisions urban India as the flywheel for India's social, economic and political transformation. And soon, along came Jana Urban Foundation, a not-for-profit social business holding company that has promoted enterprises in urban financial inclusion; Janalakshmi Financial Services, which currently serves close to 2 million urban poor families across seventy cities nationwide; and Janaadhar, an affordable housing initiative.

I feel very lucky to have Ramesh and Swati as friends and associates. They are role models for my whole family, especially for my son, Ayush, due to their focus on creating impact.

VM: What was life like before you changed course from lucrative careers to the world of non-profit organizations creating impact?

SR: We felt incredibly lucky that we had found each other and managed to get married with our families' blessings despite initial opposition. I had studied design and architecture from NID Ahmedabad and subsequently from Pratt and was eager and bright-eyed, keen to make a difference in the professional world.

RR: An early failure: not getting admission into an IIT, despite my mock test results assuring me that I would, had grounded me. I learnt that only effort is in one's control, not the outcome. That learning would come in handy in my life. Well, those early years were ones with stability and invested in pursuing excellence at our workplaces and doing well for ourselves.

VM: At what point in your life did you first think of giving back? Where did the inspiration come from?

SR: As non-resident Indian vacationers in India, once or twice a year, we met similar folks and, during weekend parties, we collectively complained about all the things that were wrong in India. It became a pattern, and those remained Friday-evening conversations. We became a little tired of that. It felt hollow. That was when Ramesh and I started discussing how we could make a real impact.

RR: While in the US, we found a mailer in our mailbox, asking us to join a park-cleaning drive on a weekend. We went there to socialize but those folks meant business! We all worked briskly and quietly and came back home. On the commuter train to work on the Monday that followed, I saw the guy who had driven the initiative. He wasn't some tree-hugging activist, just a regular banker like me. It triggered something in me.

Both: We had pursued excellence in our careers; we were satisfied. We had filled up our jewel boxes—professional skills, working with teams, being excellent at our work. We had jointly agreed on a financial goalpost. This gave us clarity in our minds around our readiness and commitment. We asked, 'Who will do it, if not us?' We were blessed with good health, we had met our financial needs, and we were still only thirty-two.

VM: Tell me about your giving-back journey.

Both: It's been a fantastic journey. Definitely tough. There were times when we didn't have time for the family. I remember that when our daughter was younger, and perhaps as a result of seeing us so consumed with our work, she would have nightmares: 'There's a monster called Janaagraha that is coming to eat us up.' One's passion may take one away from family goals for a while, but we learnt that, as long as you know you have to balance shortly after, it's fine.

The journey has been extremely enriching. It has taught us to be incredibly creative and entrepreneurial.

VM: How does Janaagraha feature in your life now?

Both: This initiative isn't a piece of our life, it's our whole life! If you look at our holiday photos, half of those feature us, the other half, storm-water drains and street-side poles! But we feel enriched. It has redefined what we think of as success. At the same time, we have focused on and balanced all our goals. We gave ourselves financial independence and made sure we didn't strip our children of the opportunities they deserve. Being back in India ensured that the kids got to know their grandparents, understand what it is to be global citizens, have an Indian cultural identity and the appreciation of life's journey that we have lived, as a family. Giving back hasn't subtracted from us; instead, it has made us whole.

VM: What has been the best part of your journey?

Both: There are so many, but overall, it's the goodwill such work attracts. So many wonderful people that one gets associated with. Such as you, Vivek, who has been so actively involved with us. The relationships and the variety of people we have connected with have been tremendous.

VM: What would be your advice to youngsters about giving back?

RR: The first thing is that you have nothing to fear. If there is a voice in your head telling you to do something for the larger good, listen to it. Don't be afraid of your parents or social circle frowning upon your plans. It will all work out. Stay tuned, listen to your own voice and start contributing in whatever way you can.

SR: Don't shut out your calling for giving back; there is a way that you can balance it with your other obligations. Women, you need not feel lesser by comparison; your voice is equally needed. Believe that your contributions are rich, necessary, different and needed. Great societies are made by average people solving public problems and adding value. Even if you give one hour a week, it's wonderful. But start right away, give time or money, whatever you can, and build on it.

THE PROOF IS IN THE PUDDING

GET A MENTOR

THIRTEEN

Lessons at Work: Get a Mentor

'Keep away from people who try to belittle your ambitions. Small people always do that, but the really great make you feel that you, too, can become great.'

—Mark Twain

I have mentored thousands of people around the world, from my driver's daughter to barely educated carpenters and landscapers to students to early and mid-career professionals to CEOs, by using the ideas covered in this book. In this chapter, I have shared feedback from some of these mentees from various backgrounds and at various stages of their life. It is nice of them to give me credit, **but the real purpose of sharing it here is to illustrate that when the ideas covered in the book have been applied, they have worked well.**

You will find one or more of the following examples closer to your situation whether you are a student, in early or mid-career, or a CEO. Hopefully, these real-life examples with significant impact on mentees inspire you to move forward.

Students—Early Career

Anant Mansingh, finance manager, Amazon, US/Singapore

My dad's mentoring helped me right from school. In high school, I had a goal of working in the area of investment management at Wall Street after graduating from college, and therefore I mapped out a plan keeping in mind my long-term career interests. Breaking this out into sub-goals meant the plan was to complete an undergraduate degree in economics/finance from a top US university. One of my target universities was the University of California, Berkeley, and following my goal with passion, proper planning and hard work got me into Berkeley. I graduated with a degree in economics and worked with an investment management firm on Wall Street in New York.

However, I soon realized it wasn't the long-term career I was looking for! I changed my professional goal and decided to go for a career in finance in a technology company. So, I set a goal to do my MBA from a school that would help me reach my goal. I got into the University of Michigan, Ross Business School. After graduating, as per my aspirations and plan, I got a job at AWS (Amazon Web Services) in finance at Amazon, Seattle.

My recent move from the US to Singapore is a decision not guided purely by a financial lens or purely from a career growth lens but from my balanced wheel of goals. The ideas shared in this book are guiding me through every phase of life.

Key Learnings: Being goal-driven is amazingly rewarding and helpful in navigating through life.

Rohan Misra, Bain Consulting, Delhi

I have known Dr Mansingh ever since I was a child. First as an affable uncle, then as an inspirational figure and finally as a voice of reason and pillar of support. He was my first mentor and introduced me to the importance of having mentors. In his usual approachable, warm and unassuming way, he drove home the point that one needs to be aware of goals one aspires to before trying to get on the journey of achieving them.

He helped me successfully navigate every part of my college journey. At the very start, when I was still confused about which course/college I should attend, he gave me a very simple yardstick to evaluate my options—choose a course of study which you are passionate about and are likely to achieve exceptional excellence in. After choosing my college and enjoying a degree of success initially, I soon faced challenges on the academic front and started having second thoughts about the path I was on.

It was during this challenging phase that Dr Mansingh sat me down and did a phenomenal goal-setting exercise with me: listing all that I wanted to achieve in the long term. With the goals and milestones clearly laid out in front of me, I found it much easier to motivate myself and passionately work hard towards realizing my potential.

I have learnt to define success in a holistic way; to focus not just on professional success but also on the relationships I cultivate and the social impact I leave behind as my legacy. The simple lessons which are covered in this book work in the most powerful way!

Key Learnings: Your wheel of goals and clarity of goals can be your Google map of life and a phenomenal motivator.

Ayush Mansingh, associate director, Social Finance, San Francisco

Goal-setting was something I started pretty early, in high school, to plan for college and career. Based on my long-term career aspirations and the subject areas I liked, I decided to pursue a business/economics degree focused on entrepreneurship. I created detailed goals of target colleges and the steps I needed to take to get into one of them. I reached my goal and got into one of my top choices in the US, Babson College, for my undergrad.

Once in college, I applied the same goal-setting technique for targeting specific courses, internships and jobs. I bagged an enviable job at the top technology company in Silicon Valley.

Later, when I wanted to pivot my career towards social impact investing, I went back to another goal-setting exercise: identifying dream jobs, target companies, and paths to reach them. It was obvious that I would need an MBA. I set a goal, did the needful and got into the MBA programme at Duke University and, following that, a career in impact investing at the prestigious Social Finance in San Francisco.

This book covers the lessons that have helped me take critical decisions and plan a life of meaningful success.

Key Learnings: Goal-setting and mentoring can help you achieve what is meaningful to you.

Rajat Swarup, senior investment analyst, YourNest VC Fund, Delhi

When I was young, I assumed that mentoring was a costly affair and that, coming from a middle-class family, I wasn't entitled to it. I took career decisions independently and learnt everything on my own. This sometimes led to failures which could have been simply avoided if I'd had access to the right mentors for guidance.

When I met Dr Mansingh on joining YourNest Venture Capital, I learnt the significance of mentors and the fact that it's our job to recognize them and reach out to them. A simple illustration given by him was that even the best sports players in the world have coaches.

Mentoring has given a big boost to my career and life goals. *I never thought it could make such a big difference!* I imbibed another learning from Dr Mansingh and made a list of inspirers and role models, professionally and personally, whom I track, to find qualities that I can acquire. I have identified mentors with whom I constantly engage to discuss career growth and other aspects.

I am now learning tennis from friends, honing my golf skills with my uncle, understanding deal flow evaluations from podcasts and books, and increasing my knowledge by actively engaging in webinar sessions. Mentors are everywhere; we have to be willing to seek them out.

Key Learnings: Everyone needs 'Four More Gods'.

Shefali Prakash, assistant director, Deloitte, London

As a child when asked what I wanted to be, it was always something wonderfully ambitious like an astronaut or the prime minister; there's no place in our beautiful minds for fear or self-doubt. But as we get older and start our professional lives, something dims this light within us. Instead of feeling as if we can take on the world, we doubt if we are good enough even in our small peer group!

Having been in that very position, I was lucky enough to have a mentor teach me how to be courageous again. He pushed me outside my comfort zone and helped me believe in myself more than I did and achieve more than I thought I could. He reminded me of the bigger picture, helped me set my own goals and, most important of all, supported me in achieving them!

Building a relationship of trust and coming from a place of genuine care and kindness, he took the time to understand my concerns and worked through dismissing them one at a time, helping me get rid of the demons in my own mind that I had unknowingly nurtured over the years.

It would be easy to pick a single decision in my life that has been impacted by my mentoring relationship, but the reality is that it has helped change my mindset and way of thinking and, in turn, touched so many aspects of my professional as well as personal life that it would be a disservice to name just one. As a young professional who has already broken barriers and can't wait to break some more, I thank you, Dr Mansingh!

I have been transformed; become braver, more confident and aligned towards meaningful goals.

Key Learnings: A mentor can make an amazing positive impact.

Mid-Career and Beyond

Ashok Karani, director, GE Healthcare, Bangalore

I have had a mentoring relationship with Dr Mansingh for close to fifteen years and have learnt a ton in different areas of life, along with amazing guidance. Let me give an example: I had two interesting job offers that I was evaluating: Company A offered 12 per cent higher compensation than my current salary, and Company B offered 10 per cent lower. As any regular person, I decided to take the offer from Company A. *Which fool would go for a lower offer?* The difference would be 22 per cent lower salary. I decided to make a call to Dr Mansingh. Without any hesitation, he said, 'Go for Company B.' I was astonished. *Why is Vivek recommending I join a company that is offering a lower salary than my current salary?* He explained that I had worked in product companies for all my career, I had competence, insights and passion for product design, and that my aspirations for long-term career growth would be better served in Company B.

I have completed many years in Company B now. My focus on developing my thinking-out-of-the-box, excellence and leadership skills has served me well. I have been promoted multiple times, done very well in my career, have designed some great products and I am a very happy person. The lesson from my journey is that when planning a career, one needs to look beyond salary. You need to know what you are good at and what you are passionate about!

This book will help you tremendously in your career and life journey. Listen to Dr Mansingh, and your life will change as mine did!

Key Learnings: Build your career around your passion, not compensation. Leadership and thinking-out-of-the-box skills can give your career a big boost.

Edward Yardumian, vice president, Dell, Austin, USA

One huge benefit of good and timely mentoring is the gift of identifying the gaps one has when aiming for long-term success. For me, it was the valuable learning that I needed to go back to school!

When working with Dr Mansingh, I was floundering initially. He led with a focus on the end state. I had never previously worked for someone with this approach and, initially, I struggled to understand it. Instead of just filling in the blanks for me, he gave me the space and coached me to figure it out. His approach forced me to think harder about the end state of our work and my role in it. Equally important, he asked about my own end state, and we discussed how I would achieve my goal of becoming an excellent leader.

Once I started thinking about the desired end state, our conversations became richer. He encouraged me to seek further education to grow as a leader. If I'd been focused only on the 'now', additional education would not have made my priority list, since its short-term value wasn't visible at that time. However, the experience from the pursuit of that education proved to be both valuable in the short term and even greater as time has passed.

The simple tips on how to get a mentor and how to leverage that relationship are priceless, and I exhort readers to apply them seriously!

Key Learnings: Focusing on the end state and developing the right skills can help you get to your destination.

Eric Prather, leader at Apple, Silicon Valley, USA

My first Silicon Valley job, just out of Stanford and at the start of the Internet boom, was with an upstart engineering services firm founded by Dr Vivek. The company was less than six months old when I joined, and I was the fifth employee.

On day one, I was handed the (seemingly overwhelming) task of driving the technical analysis and simulation of a large router for one of the biggest networking companies at that time. Vivek helped me break down that problem into a series of manageable tasks to solve. I was always encouraged to think out of the box and I realized the value of innovation. I came up with some extremely innovative designs. Becoming the best version of myself has served me (and now my direct reports) very well ever since.

Later, when I visited Vivek in Bangalore purely for mentoring, I benefited from our discussions around achieving more in life by having balanced goals around work, family, body/health, spirituality and community service. These learnings have enriched my life significantly, and I encourage readers to pay attention to the ideas shared in the book.

Key Learnings: Developing deep expertise (excellence) and aspiring for balanced goals can make life rewarding and fulfilling.

Rudramuni B., vice president, Dell, Bangalore

During my enriching tenure with Dr Vivek, I had many opportunities to learn about various topics, including being balanced, goal-driven, planning my career and giving back.

In our first meeting (I was a manager at that time), he asked me what my professional aspirations were. I told him that I wanted his job and to become the head of Dell R&D in a few years. Someone else in his place may have been annoyed, but Dr Vivek mentored me for the next five years in developing skills in leadership, planning, execution and becoming the best version of myself. When he left Dell after five years, I was ready and took up his role. Even today, I continue to practise his goal-driven techniques and meet him every year for mentoring!

Another aspect he inspired me with was that of giving back. I continued his legacy and made sure Dell R&D was at the top of the list among all Dell offices worldwide in giving back. I personally engaged with a number of charities, offering them time and financial help. Before meeting Dr Vivek, I never thought of giving back in a structured way and making a difference to the world.

I urge readers to take full advantage of this amazing book!

Key Learnings: You can get any job you want if you get ready for it.

Founders and CEOs

Dhruv Ranjan, founder and CEO, Thriwe, Delhi

In my entrepreneurial journey, I have met numerous leaders and mentors, but many of them just dismissed my ideas as unsatisfactory. Dr Mansingh was different. He spent the needed time with me to understand my personal and professional aspirations, and worked with me to create a plan to achieve them—nobody does this!

His ability to foresee the professional and personal strengths of an individual is by far the best I have seen, and it has been extremely helpful for my evolution as a professional.

I would not have succeeded without the focused hard work, solid strategy and self-evaluation that good mentoring made me do. Listening to mentors is one thing, but actually imbibing their advice is what fills the gap between partial and astounding success. My pride in entrepreneurship is established and I have improved my skills as an entrepreneur. Some of the blind spots in my approach and skills are now visible and I am working on them.

I am going to give this book to every one of my employees, associates and loved ones, to improve their life. Hope you get the inspiration I did.

Key Learnings: The mentoring ideas covered in this book can help everyone tremendously. Developing the right entrepreneurial skills and attitude is critical for the success of start-up founders.

Satish M.M., founder, Rule Zero, Bangalore

Though literally 'Vivek' means wisdom, which he has in abundance, I picked nine more words to describe him: leadership, excellence, innovation, ownership, execution, speed, integrity, entrepreneurship and mentor.

Among the many things I have learnt from him are to focus on innovation, how to bring multiple and sometimes conflicting ideas and people together to achieve a common goal, the importance of practising what you preach and mentoring.

He is a mind-boggling mentor; he invested in learning about me. When I'd start discussing a particular topic, his mind would have moved five steps ahead to figure out the good, the bad and the ugly. And if you think you have reached a goal and can relax, he throws at you your next challenge and encourages you to achieve excellence! Only an incredible mentor is capable of doing something like this. I know he celebrates my successes, big or small, and I know someone is watching my back all the time.

A good mentor gives specific advice, tailored to the mentee's needs, not generic inputs. I have gained a lot from my long-term mentoring: being goal-driven, thinking out of the box, developing leadership and deep domain expertise, perseverance, the importance of role models and sticking to one's value system. Inspired, I have made a pledge to mentor the next generation. This book will be a superb life mentor for people at any stage of their life, as these lessons have been for me.

Key Learnings: Good mentors are invaluable—get one. Excellence and leadership skills can make you a person you never thought you would ever be.

Swati Sharma, co-founder and COO, Thriwe, Delhi

I met Vivek Sir when we were a young start-up completely adrift in rocky uncertainty. Our original idea hadn't taken off as we had thought it would, our funding was just enough to survive and we were a little battered by the usual throes of entrepreneurship! I still wonder what he saw in me and our fledgling company to invest hours of his time, effort and interest over the years in us. But his belief and consistent guidance, clear strategy and becoming the best in my business became a huge motivation for us to continue striving to be a unicorn company.

While over the years I have gathered and assimilated many nuggets of advice from Vivek Sir, the one that has benefited me the most is the importance of having role models and mentors. My mentoring journey helped me build a strategic bent of mind. He taught me to find the sweet spot between optimism and realism rooted in intense scrutiny and analysis. I observed him during my discussions and picked up the simplicity of his conversations on highly complex topics; decision-making interspersed with empathy at the core; and a deep sense of family in the middle of the corporate lifecycles. As a young entrepreneur, all these direct and indirect inspirations set a great foundation for me to build my organization, career and life.

The lessons I received, which are now covered in this book, helped me improve my leadership skills, build a clear vision for my company and myself, and helped me become a passionate warrior.

Key Learnings: Get role models and mentors. One needs to be ready for getting mentored. Having a clear vision is a giant step forward in reaching your goal.

Life Coaching

Shubhra Sinha, marketing professional,
Washington, USA

Dr Vivek Mansingh is one of the most deliberate planners I know. He knew a long time ago what he wanted to achieve in life and had walked along a very self-directed, purposeful path to get to his destination. I had always admired him and his approach, but from afar. My move to California in the late nineties brought me closer to him and his family.

He guided me to balance family and career when I needed to rework my career goals to be able to spend quality time with my parents. He helped me organize my thoughts and objectives and create a solid plan. I moved to India, was able to spend a lot of time with my parents and got a challenging role at Cisco. These four years in Bangalore were formative for my career, and the daily walks with Vivek and his wife, Preeti, helped my personal growth, too, and provided a framework for solving my life's equations.

As I approached fifty, using the principles covered in this book, I created goals and a plan for myself up to ninety years of age. This helped me make one of the best decisions of my life: moving to Washington, close to my sister. Goal-setting helped me plan my finances better and enabled me to make concrete plans to pursue my passions, like classical Indian dance and travel. Life is now about all those things that light a spark of joy in me, not just job and income. Vivek helped me define the 'Marie Kondo existence' for my next forty years.

I am so happy that Vivek has decided to put all his ideas into this book. Trust me, it is invaluable if one learns from it and puts its lessons into practice. I guarantee, your career and life will be a lot more enriching.

Key Learnings: Clear life goals can help you plan all aspects of your life, and with the right focus and effort, you can achieve them all.

* * *

So, here you go: *'A truly great mentor is hard to find, difficult to part with, and impossible to forget.'*

This book could be your first mentor.

Once again, these mentees have been kind to me as a mentor; however, ***the ideas covered in the book are the core of my mentoring***. I have shared everything I know in this book, along with my experience-based learnings. Hope it helps you as much as it has scores of my mentees.

START NOW

FOURTEEN

Let the Game Begin: Start Now!

'The journey of a thousand miles begins with one step.'
—Lao Tzu

Congratulations on reading the book! Well, the real action begins now. My vision is not just to engross you (readers) but also to help you create meaningful success in your life.

Yes, you can take charge of your success and change the world if you just start with a promise to yourself. A promise in which you tell yourself that you will make action plans based on the lessons in this book before the footprints left on your mind get washed away by the humdrum of 'life as usual'. The ideas in this book may look simple to you and you may think that you have done them just by reading them; this is a big mistake. Knowing is not a substitute for taking action. If it were true, we would all have reached our goals. Do not procrastinate and plan to start some other day.

'Tomorrow is often the busiest day of the week.'
—Spanish proverb

Dr Seuss once wrote, 'The more that you read, the more things you will learn. The more that you learn, the more places you'll go.'

Get ready to go places, but first, you need to put in place the goals for your desired destinations. In a diary or on your laptop, put today's date and create a Wheel of Success as discussed in this book. To keep it simple, perhaps you can begin with just five goal categories. I'd suggest that you choose education/profession, material, health, relationships and giving-back goals.

Although I highly recommend that you start with creating long-term life goals, if you are at a stage in life where choosing long-term lifetime goals that go up to retirement seems inconceivable, start with five- to ten-year goals.

Challenge yourself: Are you thinking BIG as you are setting your aspirational goals? Are you making the world your oyster? Are you snapping all those imaginary ropes binding your thoughts and telling yourself, 'No, you can't aim so big'? Just pick up those negative thoughts as if they are scribbled on a piece of paper, crumple it and toss it in a dustbin.

Don't shrink yourself within limits; push yourself to dream big. Don't just settle for something 'manageable'. Instead, *astonish yourself with what you can dream of.* What if Dilip Kumar, yesteryear's megastar, who was once a fruit seller in Crawford Market in Mumbai, had set a 'manageable' goal like 'Sell more apples', or M.S. Dhoni, who was once a ticket collector at Kharagpur railway station set a goal like 'Become station master'? Get inspired by such stories and think of distinctive, big goals.

Then, find the words to write down each goal. Neat, precise, simple. Once you have written the goals, break them down into actionable tasks and put timelines against each task.

You are set on the path of meaningful success. Do not worry about creating a perfect plan. I have experienced that it is better to get started than wait for an impeccable plan.

Getting started is all about being conscious of every step you take towards the fulfilment of the goals. *Remember, success is the sum of small efforts that we put in every day.*

Always be mindful of the fact that you are not competing with anyone out there, you are competing with yourself; you are striving to become the best version of yourself. **Someone is already at the destination you want to reach. If you get the experience and develop the skills that person has, you will also get there.** So, focus on developing your leadership, thinking-out-of-the-box and other skills and be in the pursuit of excellence.

An honest and tough moment is setting a date for 'review'. It will be like sitting in front of a mirror and having a frank conversation. Unless you are brutally frank with yourself, you will not be able to keep the journey fruit-bearing.

Now, this journey shouldn't be like a burden. You have to give yourself validation and brownie points for reaching milestones. So, reward yourself with a treat and celebrate whenever you cross a significant step. As mentioned earlier, life's journey is as important as the destination, so be positive, joyful and enjoy the journey.

You can be a fabulous mentor to your children, nieces, nephews, colleagues and employees if you use this book as a guiding manual. Encourage them to read this book, realize their potential and achieve meaningful success. Have you heard of the Butterfly Effect? The metaphor goes: 'The flap of a butterfly's wings in Brazil can set off a tornado in Texas.' While it sounds ridiculous as a concept, it is not meant to be taken literally. The Butterfly Effect metaphor is simply meant to demonstrate that *little, insignificant events can lead to significant results over time*. Each one of us is like a butterfly, and if we move towards joy and success, in however small steps, we can create waves of joy and success through our families, institutions and communities.

Please send me your feedback, questions, concerns and success stories. I am always here as your mentor; you can reach me through my website and social media channels, the links to which have been mentioned at the end of this book.

All the best!

'You can't cross the sea merely by standing and staring at the water.'

—Rabindranath Tagore

Appendix

Guidance on Creating Your Wheel of Goals

Being goal-driven is one of the backbones of this book: if you pledge to do it with rock-solid resoluteness, meaningful success will surely come your way. This section will give you handy samples that you can use as starting points for your goal-setting exercise. Remember, they are samples for reference: they don't, by any means, prescribe that you should adhere to the categories or samples in their entirety. *You have to create your own goals.* Remember, the crux of the book is: 'Define the person you aspire to be, then become that person.'

What is the Wheel of Goals?

Simply put, it is a rounded articulation of one's desired goals based on one's aspirations. It outlines the success criteria that you are putting out there for yourself; your personally desired and unique goals.

What duration should a wheel of goals be constructed for?

As life progresses, your situations change. A student who was goal-setting to get into the best college becomes a young adult who is now planning to build a strong career and take care of a growing family or ageing parents. So, examine your life and keep making fresh short-term wheels of goals as and when needed. However, it is always great to have one wheel of goals for your entire life with the clear end state in mind.

Do I need to refer to and work on all goals on a daily basis?

It may not be possible to focus on all your goals every day, week or month. That is understandable. You might want to focus on only three to five goals in any week, month or even year.

However, if one goal category is being ignored over a longer period of time, you need to think about it and re-prioritize.

Examples of goal categories: I have used eight categories of goals for myself, as discussed in Chapter 2. However, only you can decide how you would like to define your wheel of goals and the categories you choose. If you are creating goals for the first time, I would say start with five categories.

First, create your long-term lifetime wheel of goals as discussed in Chapter 2. Once you have long-term goals laid out neatly, it's time to break them down into shorter-term goals along with timelines. Here is an example of breaking down long-term professional goals.

A.1: Breaking down long-term professional goals

One important segment of your wheel of goals will be your professional goals. You need to break those overall aspirational goals down into many short-term goals to carve a clear path for day-to-day progress towards the goals. Here is an example of how a twenty-year-old can break long-term professional goals into smaller goals.

Long-term professional goal: Build my software start-up with revenues of at least \$50–\$100 million by the age of forty (in the next twenty years).

Break down into smaller, more manageable goals:

- **Education goals:** Complete my engineering in computer science from a top college. Find a mentor and have regular sessions.

- **Career goals:** Get a job in a software company in my area of interest.
- **Next one-year goal:** Become an excellent performer in my current role and develop software development and project management skills.
- **Three-year goal:** Become a manager and develop management skills. (After becoming a manager, build skills and experience needed to become a director by making detailed development plans and working on them.)
- **Ten-year goal:** Become a director. (Develop deep technical expertise in the area of my start-up, get management and team-building experience, get exposure to business development by partnering with my sales team, join organizations like TiE to learn the basics of entrepreneurship.)
- **Twelve-year goal:** Launch my start-up, follow the ideas suggested in the chapter on 'Entrepreneurship'. Build a $5 million revenue company in the next three years.
- **Fifteen-year goal:** Now that my start-up has a revenue of $5 million, scale to take it to $50 million in the next five years.

As you can see from this example, breaking big goals down into smaller, more manageable goals makes the long-term goal practically achievable. You may not follow exactly the same path, but such goals will give you amazing clarity and become your professional road map.

Similarly, break down your goals in other categories into more manageable milestones and track yourself to make sure you are moving forward.

A.2: Example of short-term goals for students (Grades 9–12)

As students reach senior grades, they need to start figuring out what they wish to specialize in with their career choices in mind. At the same time, they need their goals to be in a wheel that captures all aspects, not just studies.

Here is a sample wheel of goals for a student in Grade 9 interested in pursuing an engineering/medical/finance/law career. (For other professions, the goals can be modified accordingly.)

- **Education goals:** Focus on good grades in the next four years and build a solid understanding of concepts to apply to engineering/medical/finance/law colleges after Grade 12. Target the best colleges and universities you can enter. With that in mind, aim to be in the top 10–20 per cent of the class, and have a solid preparation for college/university entrance exams. Participate in debate, essay and other such competitions.
- **Health goals:** Exercise (running, jogging, kick-boxing, spinning or any such brisk activity) for thirty

minutes every day. Play some sport in your school or state junior team.

- **Relationship goals:** Practise music or play badminton with your parents every week. Go hiking or for a picnic with your family once a month.
- **Giving-back goals:** Pick a cause that you care about and volunteer at an institution that is addressing it. Teach the maid's son twice a week or volunteer at an orphanage.
- **Fun goals:** Play cricket or other sports with friends. Doodle in an art journal. Learn cooking, painting, etc.

A.3: Example of short-term goals for university students

Once graduation is in sight, students have a clearer picture of which stream they'd like to further specialize in. One scans the job market and eyes jobs that are in line with one's aspirations. How does a student make a fresh wheel of goals in this phase of life? Here is an example of a wheel of goals for a student completing an engineering undergraduate degree and interested in a job/career in artificial intelligence. (Students in other disciplines can use the following example to create professional goals that are relevant to them.)

- **Education goals:** Graduate with good grades, focus on learning, especially AI courses, and other related fields. Do internships in the AI area.

- **Professional goals:** Identify the top companies for AI, understand the application process and career progression of AI careers, target an AI job in a top company, get a mentor, read two books on AI, and one on interviewing techniques. Listen to and learn AI from webinars and podcasts.
- **Health goals:** Play some sport in your college team. Exercise three times a week at the college gym or on the jogging track. Learn meditation and deep-breathing techniques.
- **Relationship goals:** Build strong relationships with friends, surround yourself with friends that bring positive energy. Spend time with parents and siblings when at home.
- **Giving-back goals:** Volunteer for a charity at college, reach out to college staff and their children who might need help.
- **Fun goals:** Play cricket. Watch a movie every week. Organize a karaoke evening with friends every month. Take up a baking course.

A.4: Example of short-term goals for university students interested in creating their own start-up right after college

The new India offers wonderful opportunities for youngsters to create start-ups and hence, instead of working for someone else, create jobs for others. If you have the entrepreneurial itch and feel that the world of start-ups is your true calling, here is a sample wheel of goals for you.

- **Educational goals:** Graduate with good grades, focus on learning deeply in your domain of entrepreneurial interest, do a project/internship in the area of interest for your start-up ideally at a start-up. Find a mentor and have regular sessions.
- **Professional goals:** Learn about start-ups and start creating a business plan. Join an organization like TiE to learn about various aspects of start-ups. Get a mentor and keenly scrutinize the suggestions shared in the chapter on 'Entrepreneurship' in this book. Launch the start-up just after graduation.
- **Health goals:** Exercise thrice a week using any method of choice: running, cycling, Zumba, yoga, outdoor games and so on.
- **Relationship goals:** Build strong relationships with friends, surround yourself with friends who bring positive energy. Spend time with parents and siblings when home.
- **Giving-back goals:** Volunteer for a charity at college, teach a needy staff member a life skill.
- **Fun goals:** Play cricket. Watch a movie every week. Learn soap-making. Join an improv class.

A.5. Example of short-term goals for professionals in early career (one to three years)

Starting a job is an exhilarating experience. You experience a sense of independence and the joy of earning money. You make new friends and build a network. Each accomplishment is a happy moment. This period is a time when you can possibly lose focus on goal-setting and feel 'I have arrived'. To avoid making this mistake, refer to your long-term wheel of goals again and make an aligned, fresh short-term wheel of goals for yourself.

Here is an example:

- **Professional goals:** Become a manager responsible for a team. Understand career progression in the field of your interest, and focus on skill development through professional courses and experiences.
- **Educational goals:** Target top-tier institutions for further education or special courses if needed. Read five books on the field of your interest to keep up to date and continue to learn. Listen to one or more podcasts a month and make notes on key points. Find a mentor and have regular sessions.
- **Financial goals:** Begin to support parents/other family (as required). Begin saving and investing with clear goals. Research carefully on saving schemes and invest wisely.

- **Material goals:** Buy a motorbike. Get membership to an athletic club.
- **Health goals:** Exercise every day for forty-five minutes using any method of choice. Team sports at work, like basketball after work, help to build relationships while giving you a good workout!
- **Spiritual goals:** At this stage of life, starting to discover your life's purpose and definition of a meaningful life is important. Use meditation and prayer fifteen minutes a day to explore oneness of mind and body.
- **Relationship goals:** Support and build strong relationships with family, build a strong group of genuine friends. Start thinking about marriage and family.
- **Fun goals:** Go on vacation every year for seven days with family. Start a terrace garden. Learn a new craft.
- **Giving-back goals:** Volunteer/donate to charity, sponsor the education of lesser privileged kids.

A.6. Example of goals for mid- to senior-level professionals

At this point in your career, you will be extremely busy in your professional activities. It is easy to lose focus on balanced goals. To avoid making this mistake, refer to your long-term wheel of goals again and make an aligned fresh wheel of goals for yourself.

- **Career goals:** Become a VP/SVP/CEO in the next ten to fifteen years. Focus on getting the right experiences to be ready for this career progression. Develop personal excellence, thinking-out-of-the-box and leadership skills as you progress through this path. Make short-term goals based on milestones that will help you build these critical success skills. Achieve excellence in your job, take on difficult projects, and come up with new ideas to solve customer problems. In a nutshell, get ready for the role you are seeking.

- **Educational goals:** Complete executive education degree from a good institution. Do specialized courses in your area to keep current. Read twenty books in your field of interest to keep up to date and continue to learn. Identify people who inspire you and your role models, read their work and learn from them as much as possible. Find a mentor and have regular sessions.

- **Financial goals:** Have a net worth of Rs 1 or 5 or 10 crore. Begin to support parents/other family (as required). Begin saving and investing with clear goals.

- **Material goals:** Buy an SUV/luxury car/apartment/house. Get membership to a club.

- **Health goals:** Exercise every day for forty-five minutes using any method of choice.

- **Relationship goals:** Spend quality time with your spouse, children, parents and extended family. Do some interesting projects with your children and mentor them. Build a strong group of genuine friends and a professional network.

- **Spiritual goals:** Meditation and/or prayer fifteen to thirty minutes every or every other day.
- **Fun goals:** Go on vacation every six months or year for seven days with family. Start a terrace garden. Learn a new craft. Watch a movie every week. Read books.
- **Giving-back goals:** Volunteer/donate to charity, sponsor the education of three less privileged kids, extend medical care to ten less fortunate people; whatever suits you.

A.7: Example of wheel of goals for people retired from their primary job

Welcome to the golden years of your life—a time to reap the benefits of your hard work. Research shows that retirees who stay somewhat active with planned activities tend to be happier than those who don't. Here is a sample wheel of goals for you for the next five to ten years.

- **Play second innings:** Health permitting, offer the benefit of your knowledge and experience to for-profit and non-profit institutions as an adviser or consultant.
- **Giving-back goals:** Mentor fifty youngsters including your grandchildren, educate five less

privileged, extend medical care to ten less fortunate, contribute through a Rotary Club or NGO of choice.

- **Financial goals:** Manage your financial assets well and plan to live within your means. But use some of your savings to do things that you always wanted to do, but couldn't due to other financial needs.
- **Health goals:** Recalibrate your weight goal, eat age-appropriate healthy food and do light exercises for sixty minutes thrice a week.
- **Spiritual goals:** Now that you have more time on your hands, volunteer at the temple or your chosen place of worship, converse with the Almighty through prayer or meditation.
- **Relationship goals:** Spend time with your children, grandchildren and friends.
- **Fun goals:** Travel to one new country every year, go golfing twice a week, make an online page to display your craft work, learn Tai Chi, learn to cook a new cuisine. Read books, or watch movies and sports events.

* * *

I hope these samples of wheels of goals will be useful in getting you started and that at least one of these is close to your current situation. Do not procrastinate, start your wheel of goals today. All you need is the inner strength for self-governance. *Write down your goals at every stage of life.* Challenge yourself, give the best you have. The world will be at your feet, and you will achieve meaningful success, fulfilment and happiness.

Questions and Ongoing Mentoring

Please follow me on one or more of the social media channels mentioned below. I already mentor many people through these channels.
LinkedIn: Dr Vivek Mansingh (linkedin.com/in/dr-vivek-mansingh-530a3a)
Instagram: TheMeaningfulSuccess
Facebook: Vivek Mansingh
Twitter: @MansinghVivek

Congratulations on reading the book. Do you have any questions?

Please feel free to contact us using one of my social media channels or my website mentioned below:

Website: www.vivekmansingh.com

One of my mentees or I will answer your questions individually or as a group.

There is no charge or obligation for online mentoring.

My dream is to 'Mentor A Million' young people and have a positive impact on them.

Acknowledgements

Writing this book has been the culmination of a dream that I have nursed for decades. The dream to mentor not one, not ten, not hundreds, but a million young people. The journey has been more rewarding than I could have ever imagined.

None of this would have been possible without Rachna Thakurdas Singh, who came onboard not only as co-author but a co-owner of my vision and purpose. Our sessions devoted to crafting this book were delightful.

A big thanks to Suresh Huidrom for all the amazing sketches he created for the book. He is an internationally acclaimed artist and architect who has won numerous awards in India, the US, the UK and Singapore, and is one of the most creative persons I know.

I am deeply indebted to the great masters of meaningful success—Ratan Tata, Narayana Murthy, Sadhguru Ji, John Chambers, Kiran Mazumdar-Shaw, Dr Devi Shetty, Rahul Dravid, Prakash Padukone, Vinita

Bali, Vani Kola, Ramesh and Swati Ramanathan—who came forth so graciously to share lessons from their lives for this book. Their wisdom has enhanced the message of the book manifold.

There are so many smart young folks whom I mentor, and many have come forward to help in various phases of putting this book together. Some have shared bytes from their lives to demonstrate how lessons from this book have worked for them. I am immensely grateful to them: Anant Mansingh, Ashok Kirani, Ayush Mansingh, Dhruv Ranjan Verma, Edward Yardumian, Eric Prather, Rajat Swarup, Rohan Misra, Rudramuni B., Satish M.M., Shefali Prakash, Shubhra Sinha, Sneh Vaswani, Sujay Dutta and Swati Sharma.

I am so thankful to my dear friend Jija Hari Singh, for her constant encouragement and help. I must make a special mention of Tara Nair, Ajay Bharadwaj, Sudhir Sethi, Dr Akshai Mansingh and Dr Ravi Prakash for helping me with the connects I needed.

Ellen Lupu for editorial inputs. Shinin Preeth for creative ideas for the cover design. Aisha Singh, Sanjay Jha, Anu John, Ravin Krishna, Nandalal and Gagan Arora for social media and website help. Jaya Kumar, CEO, Toonz Media Group, who offered his generous help with the book website and social media.

To my publisher Penguin Random House India represented by CEO Gaurav Srinagesh, his leadership team and amazing editor Manish Kumar for reposing faith in this book and our fruitful sessions on giving it its final shape.

To my family for their support and for reviewing the book and giving me invaluable feedback. My wife, Preeti, for never once complaining about my single-minded focus on the book and the late nights that I spent writing it. Without her support, I would not have achieved meaningful success.

To my house help, Paltu, who served me hundreds of cups of tea while I was writing this book.

I want to thank god most of all, because without god's help and guidance, I wouldn't have walked down a path of meaningful success and penned it down.